Beyond the ADHD Label

One Mother's Struggle for Change

Beyond the ADHD Label

One Mother's Struggle for Change

By

Paula Burgess

Copyright © 2016 Paula Burgess
Beyond the Maze
WEB: www.beyondthemaze.com.au

First published 2016
MJL Publications
17 Spencer Avenue
Deception Bay QLD 4508
Australia
WEB: www.mjlpublications.com.au

Editing Services Kylee Bristow
Book Cover by Liane Barker
Layout by Alex Fay

All rights reserved. Without limiting the rights under copyright reserved above, no part of this publication may be reproduced, stored in or introduced in to a database and retrieval system, or transmitted in any form or by any means (electronic, mechanical, photocopying, recording or otherwise) without the prior written permission of both the owner of the copyright and the above publishers.

Although some of the information in this book pertains to matters of health and personal development, it is for information purposes only and it is not intended to replace medical advice in any way, shape or form. If you choose to use any of the information in this book the publisher will assume no responsibility for your actions.

ISBN# 978-0-9942205-3-0

Dedicated to my beautiful, quirky, clever little boy who I love more every day and who inspires me to keep going on my own personal journey to help the world see the positives in ADHD.

Foreword

This is a story about parenting and about being an imperfect parent.

As a child psychiatrist, I spend every day working with imperfect parents. I am one myself! No parent is perfect, but it takes a brave person to admit this, let alone write a book about their experience. Paula has done just this in the hope that other families can learn from her story.

Paula first came to see me for advice about her son, JB. She explained that JB had been expelled from day care the previous year and, since starting school, had been having difficulties in the classroom and on the playground due to his impulsive behaviour.

In my first session with JB, we talked about all the things he liked (Lego and spaghetti) and disliked (broccoli and pumpkin), but the conversation was challenging as JB couldn't sit still or focus. He ran down the hallway so quickly that he tripped over his feet. A game of stacking blocks ended in frustration as he was so impulsive and fidgety that his tower kept toppling over. After a few sessions, it was quite clear to me that JB had ADHD.

Paula and I discussed various treatment options, including medication. Her first question was the same one most parents ask me: 'Will medication turn my child into a zombie?' Medication can be a contentious and difficult issue for many families, and Paula's story will help any parent who has considered medicating their child for emotional or behavioural difficulties.

Parenting is hard work and most of us have had days we'd rather forget. Paula gives a raw and honest account of the tears and the tantrums. She describes the heartbreak of seeing her child alone and excluded from friends. Many of us can relate to her story of feeling overwhelmed and crying to herself in the car. Paula reminds us that no parent is perfect. All parents make mistakes and have regrets.

So while Paula has written her book specifically about parenting a child with ADHD, her story will resonate with *every* parent because, above all, this is a story about a mother's love for her child.

Dr Laura Hamilton - BSc, MBBS (Hons), FRANZCP, Cert. Child Adol. Psych, Cert. Cons. Liaison Psych.

Dr Laura Hamilton is a psychiatrist with advanced training in both Child and Adolescent Psychiatry and Consultation Liaison Psychiatry. Dr Hamilton enjoys working with children and their families to help young people develop their strengths and learn to manage distress effectively. She has a collaborative approach to treatment that involves liaising with other health care providers, including psychologists, GPs and paediatricians.

Contents

Foreword 7
Acknowledgments 13
About the author 15
Introduction 19
ADHD – what it really is 23
My story 31
ADHD in society 53
Having friends (or not) 65
ADHD and your relationship 71
To medicate or not medicate 87
The food question 105
School issues 113
Specialists 131
Programs and strategies 153
Doggie therapy 171
Mindset 179
Where are we now? 189
Beyond the Maze 197
Notes 199

Acknowledgments

Firstly, I would like to dedicate this book to my beautiful son who is seven years old at the time of writing. He is my only child and one that I fought very hard to make a part of my life.

My son, although you have been diagnosed with ADHD—which can sometimes be a very hard and trying road—I have decided to look at this diagnosis as a good thing and not allow you to be labelled negatively.

You have made me re-evaluate my life and live it how I choose by making a difference for other people on the same journey.

You are the light of my life; you are the most charismatic, smart, beautiful boy I have ever met. You have made a massive change in my life so far and I am sure you will continue to do so.

I love you with all of my heart!

I love you to infinity and beyond!

I would also like to acknowledge my friends and family who have believed in my ability to make this possible:

Beyond the ADHD Label
One Mother's Struggle for Change

To my husband who, in the beginning, was wary of the path I'd chosen to empower people to see the good in ADHD. Now he is slowly seeing the positives, and my passion and desire, and has put his concerns aside to support me on this road.

To my wonderful mother who has been there every step of the way and supported me in every way she can. When things get tough, she just knows when to step in and take the reins to give me a break. She has an unbreakable bond with my son because of it.

To my wonderful stepchildren and friends—particularly Angela, Kelly and Bec—who have believed in me from the beginning, and reminded me of my passion and abilities as a parent when things have been tough. Without their belief in me, I would be a heap on the floor still trying to deal with it all instead of choosing to be positive and inspire others.

About the author

I'm Paula, a mum of four children—three stepchildren and one of my own—and now a step-grandma ('Grammy') to two beautiful boys. I live in Deception Bay in Queensland, Australia, on a property with my husband and son. My parents live on the same block in a separate residence.

From a young age, I knew I didn't want children. Then I met my husband and discovered that most of the boys on his side of the family live with ADHD. I knew I definitely didn't have the patience for a child living with ADHD.

However, all that changed at about 30 when I decided I would one day like a child of my own. A few years later, my son was born.

To my surprise, I found that I *did* actually have the patience to help my son, JB, and ended up changing my life completely to help him through his own.

Recently, I started a business called Beyond the Maze to support other parents of children living with ADHD. I speak to people and present at events to get ADHD more widely

Beyond the ADHD Label
One Mother's Struggle for Change

accepted and understood in society. I also run courses and webinars, write books, run retreats and have several other big—somewhat huge—future goals to provide support for ADHD.

My life has changed immensely since my son has come into it. I've gone from being a career-driven financial planner with no intention of ever giving up work to a devoted mother, speaker, author and home business owner who wakes up every day hoping to spread the word about ADHD.

This book is about my journey with ADHD (thus far!)—including all the scary, difficult, not-so-pretty bits—and how you can work through the tough times too. I have many more books in my head, so you have plenty more support to come as well.

You can find me at:

- www.beyondthemaze.com.au
- www.facebook.com.au/adhdbeyondthemaze.

My hope is that, by honestly sharing our stories and experiences, we can all help each other on our amazing journeys. Thanks for joining me on mine.

About the author

~ Paula Burgess

Beyond the ADHD Label
One Mother's Struggle for Change

Introduction

When it comes to ADHD, there are many different opinions—and many of those opinions can be pretty uneducated about the true nature of ADHD. Once upon a time, I was one of those people with a lot of those opinions. Before my son was diagnosed, I really didn't understand the diagnosis in its true form.

My adult stepson also lives with ADHD, as do most of the boys in my husband's family. Interestingly, not the girls. So I always suspected that, if we had a male child, he would probably have it too. As a result, we tried everything to have a girl!

However, after reading many books on different ways to conceive girls, including what foods to eat and what clothes to wear, we were blessed with a beautiful boy. (And, in truth, I look back now and wonder what I would've done with a girl, as I'm a bit of a tomboy myself.)

At least having ADHD in the family gave us a good knowledge of what to look for. So the minute we started having problems

Beyond the ADHD Label
One Mother's Struggle for Change

in day care and saw the signs, we jumped on it and got JB the help he needed.

However, for those first few years, I actually fought the ADHD diagnosis. I thought I knew enough about it to know that he didn't live with it. After all, he was nothing like his older brother had been at his age (from the stories the family had told me). He could sit and play with blocks or colour in a book for hours on end. He wasn't running around the house tearing up the place.

So I spent the next four years saying 'The specialists don't know what they're talking about' and 'My son does not have ADHD'.

But the problems didn't go away and I started to wonder. I decided to study more about it and only then did I finally accept that JB did live with ADHD. I came to understand that he could play with blocks and colour in books because these things interested him—he was hyperfocused on these activities rather than hyperactive (as many people misunderstand ADHD to be).

Introduction

From then on, I made it my mission to learn everything I could. And, as I did, I decided to write this book to help other parents on the same journey.

If you are on this amazing journey, I hope you know it's not a lonely one. There are plenty of parents like us in the world dealing with the same thing.

Daily life with these kids can be really hard and it's easy to get bogged down with the negative things happening in their life. The negativity can start affecting you as a parent mentally and physically. It certainly has for me at times.

But I've found that life is a lot easier to deal with when I can find the good in it.

I strongly urge you to seek some help for yourself if you feel you're not coping, as it is a hard road and no one will tell you otherwise. You must remember that this is nothing you've done wrong; it's just the way their brain functions, which can be absolutely amazing—but also incredibly difficult.

Feel free to jump onto my website, Beyond the Maze, and drop me a line or read my blogs. I run support groups on Facebook at www.facebook.com.au/adhdbeyondthemaze if you'd like to join. I also run physical support groups if you're

Beyond the ADHD Label
One Mother's Struggle for Change

in outer north Brisbane (soon to be rolled out across Australia).

I hope that, by reading my story, you might relate to it and feel reassured that someone out there is going through the same thing as you.

ADHD – what it really is

ADHD defined–sort of!

Attention Deficit Hyperactivity Disorder (ADHD). Speak to the professionals and they'll tell you it's a complex disorder and there's still lots more to learn about it. It can present differently for different people, so diagnosing ADHD can be a complex process.

The ADD Coach Academy (ADDCA) defines ADHD as follows[1]:

> *Attention Deficit Hyperactivity Disorder is a neurobiological condition that affects children and adults who consistently experience challenges in impulsivity, hyperactivity, and the ability to pay attention (distractibility). You will hear the term "executive functioning" used to describe the cognitive abilities that challenge those with ADHD - the brain is inefficient when it comes to planning, organization, working memory, and self-*

Beyond the ADHD Label
One Mother's Struggle for Change

regulation. These will show up in your clients as difficulty paying attention, controlling impulses, regulating their emotions and emotional responses, taking consistent actions, remembering things, and following through.

Generally, there are two types of ADHD: inattentive and hyperactive-impulsive. Your child may live with one or a mix of both. Following are the most common traits of these ADHD types:

Inattention:

(a) *Often fails to give close attention to details or makes careless mistakes in schoolwork, work, or other activities*

(b) *Often has difficulty sustaining attention in tasks or play activities*

(c) *Often does not seem to listen when spoken to directly*

(d) *Often does not follow through on instructions and fails to finish schoolwork, chores, or duties in the workplace (not due to oppositional behaviour or failure to understand instructions)*

ADHD – what it really is

(e) Often has difficulty organizing tasks and activities

(f) Often avoids, dislikes, or is reluctant to engage in tasks that require sustained mental effort (such as schoolwork or homework)

(g) Often loses things necessary for tasks or activities (e.g., toys, school assignments, pencils, books, or tools)

(h) Is often easily distracted by extraneous stimuli

(i) Is often forgetful in daily activities

Hyperactivity:

(a) Often fidgets with hands or feet or squirms in seat

(b) Often leaves seat in classroom or in other situations in which remaining seated is expected

(c) Often runs about or climbs excessively in situations in which it is inappropriate (in adolescents or adults, may be limited to subjective feelings of restlessness)

(d) Often has difficulty playing or engaging in leisure activities quietly

(e) Is often "on the go" or often acts as if "driven by a motor"

(f) Often talks excessively

Beyond the ADHD Label
One Mother's Struggle for Change

Impulsivity:

(a) *Often blurts out answers before questions have been completed*

(b) *Often has difficulty waiting turn*

(c) *Often interrupts or intrudes on others (e.g., butts into conversations or games)*

Of course, in addition to these traits, there are other criteria that a specialist will use to diagnose ADHD. But these lists give you a general idea of what you're dealing with.

Looking at these lists, I wonder if the label Attention Deficit Hyperactivity Disorder may send an incorrect message—particularly the use of the term 'hyperactivity'. Given that there are several types of this disorder, hyperactivity shouldn't necessarily be part of that definition. These children could be 'hyper-anything', including hyperfocused, as I mentioned earlier.

What we do know is that anyone who lives with ADHD has a difference about them. Each person has their own quirks and one person's presentation of ADHD isn't exactly like another.

ADHD – what it really is

Getting beyond the label

The label Attention Deficit Hyperactivity Disorder makes it sound like a truly negative thing—like the child is missing something and they can't function in the everyday world. If you're a parent of a child living with ADHD, you know this is far from the truth.

Is it really a 'disorder'? According to the medical definition it is, but I personally don't think so. Calling ADHD a disorder suggests there's something *wrong* with our children, when really they just think differently and, therefore, don't conform to society. Many people who don't conform to society have achieved great things. They have even been called geniuses!

In his book, *Staying Focused in a Hyper World: Book 1; Natural Solutions for ADHD, Memory and Brain Performance*, Dr John Gray states[2]:

> *In most cases, there is no actual deficit of attention at all. Instead, there is an inability to allocate attention appropriately. ADHD children that are inattentive, distracted or "spaced out" are unable to allocate their attention to what*

Beyond the ADHD Label
One Mother's Struggle for Change

their teachers are saying; instead they are focused on a daydream. Other ADHD children that are hyperactive, impulsive or restless are also unable to focus on the teacher but for different reasons. They are simply not that interested in what the teacher is saying. They would rather be somewhere else. They can't sit still in class but they can certainly sit still in front of a TV or video game.

If we look past the negative behaviours and deal with them as they arise, we can see our children for who they really are: people who are superfocused on the things that interest them. Allow them to do what's interesting for *them* and they'll change the world! They'll be caring when they really feel the need to look after someone and they'll have passion when they believe in something.

These are generally wonderful children. With the right guidance, they can achieve anything they're interested in. It's just a matter of finding that interest and helping them direct their lives in that way.

ADHD – what it really is

Just like some of the brilliant people who have done great things in this world who live with ADHD every day. Just google all the famous people and entrepreneurs of today and throughout history who are reported to have been diagnosed with ADHD but haven't let that stop them.

These people all have a story and so does your child. And so do you. By speaking out and sharing our stories, we can help each other learn more about ADHD, get through the tough times and uncover the gifts inside our children.

I'll start by telling you my story—the good, the bad and the just plain ridiculous. Perhaps something will resonate with you. And maybe, someday, I'll get to hear your story too.

Beyond the ADHD Label
One Mother's Struggle for Change

My story

As I take you through my journey in this book, I hope you can learn from what we've already done and that it helps you in living with a child with ADHD. And, importantly, I hope that you'll realise you're never alone.

Over time, I've learned to get over my fear of asking for help. Recently, I've even sourced my own psychologist to help me though the tough times. And I've built a business around providing support for all of us wanting to learn more and give our gifted children the best possible life.

But it wasn't always like this for me. And, in the beginning, it was heartbreakingly difficult. Some days were so long and hard, I wasn't sure I'd get through them in one piece. Now I'll tell you a bit about that time.

Here is my story...

The decision

The year was 2004 and it was my 30th birthday. I'd gathered the family for lunch at an Italian restaurant about 20 minutes from home. My husband and I drove ourselves to the

Beyond the ADHD Label
One Mother's Struggle for Change

restaurant. And, to this day, I can still remember the exact location on our car ride where I suddenly blurted out, 'Well, I'm 30 now, so I'd better decide whether I want a child or not'. I think my husband nearly crashed the car!

You see, my husband is 15 years older than me and we'd been together for 10 years at that point. And I'd never wanted children. He had three kids from a previous marriage who made him very happy and, although I sometimes found it challenging, I enjoyed being a stepmum. Also, ADHD was rampant in my husband's family, which made the question of having a child more complicated.

After that car ride and over the next four years, we discussed it *a lot* until finally the decision was made—we would have a child together. I then read every book available about how to conceive a girl, as the girls in his family didn't live with ADHD.

But, when I was 20 weeks pregnant, I was told I was having a boy. So clearly those books didn't work!

This was quite a shock to me—what would I do with a boy? Well, it turns out, quite a lot. And this boy has changed my life.

My story

The calm before the storm

JB was the best baby a parent could ask for. Like most new mums, I was besotted. He fed well and slept perfectly, and I was the most rested mother around. In fact, I even found myself a little bored—I'd organised my home to the point of categorising my DVDs and was begging my employer to give me work to do from home!

You see, I was a career woman at heart—a qualified financial planner—and I didn't want to give up my career because I'd had a child. I wanted both. So I ended up back at work when JB was 15 weeks old. I won't say I wasn't heartbroken at leaving him; in fact, I spent most of the first day back at work crying.

The first two years of JB's life went relatively smoothly and he charmed the women at his day care centre. Everyone loved him and he was the light of everyone's life, especially his siblings and other family members.

Then, when JB was three years old, we noticed a change—something other than the normal toddler changes. That's when our journey started.

The storm

One day, the day care called me in for a meeting. They told me JB wasn't getting on well with his peers and, in fact, was being quite nasty. There were four boys who had teamed up to pick on other kids and JB was a leader. It seems he'd formed himself a little gang at just three years of age!

We knew this was serious, as he couldn't go around hurting other children. But how do you get that through to a three year old? We tried everything we could think of but nothing worked. It seemed to be some kind of behavioural issue, but we couldn't pinpoint what was causing it. So the search for specialists began.

I researched the best doctor for him and found one who had previously worked at the Sydney Children's Hospital. I also researched how diet might be affecting him but only on a small scale. We removed all numbers (preservatives and additives) from his diet and sourced an amazing phone app called The Chemical Maze[3] so I could make better food choices.

However, it wasn't enough and the behaviour remained. Given the family's genetics, we took this seriously and started looking for early intervention to help with his social behaviour. At a mere three years of age, JB got his own psychologist.

At this point, I realised that the road was going to be long. I suspected that working full time for an employer may not be feasible much longer and the idea of having my own business began to form.

Expelled from day care

It was December 2012 and JB was four years old. After many meetings with day care, I was called into the office one more time. I think I knew what was coming. I walked in to see a teacher and the director. They had a few nice words to say but then the axe fell quickly: 'Paula, we're going to have to ask you to leave.'

At that moment, my world fell apart. My four-year-old son was being expelled. From day care! Whose child gets expelled from day care?

They told me that, for the next four weeks, JB would be allowed to attend day care for two out of his four days. Then he would have to go elsewhere. My mind was reeling. How would JB cope with this kind of change? And what was I supposed to do on the other two days when I worked full time?

I went straight back to work afterwards, which probably wasn't a great idea, as I ended up telling my boss about it while crying my eyes out. Fortunately, I had an amazing, understanding employer who allowed me to work from home those two days a week that I now had JB. First battle sorted.

However, finding another day care wasn't easy. He had so many social problems that we had to choose the right day care for him and ensure the transition wouldn't put him back further. In the end, we stayed with the same company for familiarity, but at a different centre.

I worried about how this change of routine would affect JB, considering just driving a different way to day care could set off a meltdown. How would we manage changing a day care that he'd attended for three-and-a-half years?

Yes, it was a stressful time—for him and for us. But it was also the best move we could have made, as he ended up with the best teacher he could have had.

My story

Searching for solutions

Getting expelled from day care changed the game and we started getting the help we needed. JB's doctor and psychologist started taking more notice and I got much more verbal about what needed to happen. We investigated various solutions.

Early Learning Development Program

A friend told me about the Early Childhood Learning Development Program at the local special school. I knew it was something JB needed to be in, so I made a lot of noise to the right people to find out how to get in.

We were told that JB wouldn't be socially ready for school the following year, though he was more than ready academically. But I wasn't having that!

I called a meeting with the psychologist to find out how to get into this program. Then I spent the next month pushing for appointments with the school and psychologist so we could get him accepted. Finally he was.

Beyond the ADHD Label
One Mother's Struggle for Change

Dietician

We then sourced a dietician to address JB's diet. We removed all preservatives, numbers, colours, amines and salicylates, stripping his diet back to boring, bland meals and making absolutely everything from scratch.

Once we had a baseline to work from, we gradually reintroduced food items to see what he responded to. The dietician said JB's behaviour indicated he may be amine sensitive or intolerant. But reintroducing salicylates, found in lots of fruits, elicited no reaction, so this wasn't the issue.

We then reintroduced amines, found in some fruits, chocolate, bread and other items. We started with bread and bananas. He loved bananas, so giving him three to four a day was no problem—until mid-morning on day three when day care called to say JB had smashed a computer!

I called the dietician and we stopped bananas immediately (which was really hard given how much he loved them). We never needed to introduce the chocolate. The dietician said that JB's reaction on day three showed he was a slow responder to amines. So if he went to a friend's house and had normal bread, he would be unlikely to react; but if he had many days of bread, he would probably react.

Of course this wasn't the end of the behaviour issues, but we did learn to control some behaviours with diet, which we still do today. (Read more about our journey with food later in the book.)

Paediatrician

We then invested in a paediatrician, who diagnosed him with Oppositional Defiant Disorder after seeing him for only two sessions for about 30 minutes and handing me a script for drugs.

I needed more answers than just medication. Thankfully, our GP and psychologist agreed.

(Read more about our journey with specialists, and strategies and programs, later in the book.)

I can't have a job!

Considering everything happening with JB and suspecting the long road ahead of us, I knew that working for someone was going to get very hard very soon. So I decided to start my own business to get some flexibility and avoid becoming the world's worst employee.

My husband almost had a heart attack when I told him—probably because we had two mortgages at the time. But we both knew this was the only way I could support JB completely and do all the things we needed to do.

We developed a plan that seems crazy now that I look back on it. I would spend the next 12 months working full time, start my business part time, get clients, juggle the part-time special school program and day care, research new strategies, maintain a diet that required everything to be made from scratch and every meal cooked (no takeaways allowed!) and take JB to specialist appointments.

I don't know how I survived that year, but somehow I did. And, eventually, I got a business off the ground so I could leave my full-time job around the same time school started. I was ready for the next part of our lives to begin.

School time

Finding a school

By the time JB was five, I had the OK for him to go to school and the interviews began.

My story

A child like JB can't go to any old school and, if your child is the same, I recommend taking the time to be extremely honest with schools to ensure they know what they're dealing with (and are equipped to deal with them!).

You may not want to tell the school about your child's problems; but if you're upfront and honest, they can also be honest about whether they can provide an education for your child. There's no point putting a child into a school that can't work for them—you'll just end up with suspensions and/or expulsions, which will do the child no good.

Eventually we found an amazing Catholic school that was extremely thorough. They assessed him at the day care and the special school as well. They had three meetings with us before deciding they could take him if we supported them and continued to work with a psychologist. (At that stage, they didn't know me or just how much support they would get from me.)

Beyond the ADHD Label
One Mother's Struggle for Change

We went through the transition process and JB was ready to start school.

Prep class started in January and we were very apprehensive about how JB would handle it. We got sign off for funding, so he had support in his classroom and I think we received the most equipped Prep teacher ever. She was amazing.

Putting a team together

That year held some massive learning curves for everyone. At the start, we wondered, 'How will he fit into a school environment? Is he ahead of other children because he is quite clever but also behind socially? How will the school handle this?'

We all worked together to put systems in place. I bought sensory items for him; we continued to follow the diet; we saw the psychologist; and we even worked with the occupational therapist that the school recommended. That last one didn't really work for us, but we took the information she gave us and did what we needed to do.

By the third term, things had escalated and problems were starting to arise. The school recommended a child psychiatrist as well. Interestingly, at no time was ADHD mentioned; only

My story

ASD (Autism Spectrum Disorder) and ODD (Oppositional Defiant Disorder).

By now, we had so many specialists in our corner that no one really agreed on what JB had. They did agree on one thing—he was 'an interesting little fellow' who didn't really fit one mould. As you can imagine, that didn't help at all. We even paid for cognitive assessment to perhaps help him through school, but that only told us he was 18 months ahead intellectually and 18 months behind socially—a difficult combination for the school to work with.

So I went with the school guidance counsellor to find out if this child psychiatrist could help. I voiced my concerns about medicating my five-year-old son, as I felt it wasn't time to visit this option because we hadn't tried everything yet. She agreed. We discussed our action plan and then agreed to use her as a case manager who would give everyone directions for what needed to be done.

With all this in place, we made it through Prep. But then came Year 1.

Beyond the ADHD Label
One Mother's Struggle for Change

Our (short) journey with medication

We really thought Year 1 would be easy compared with Prep. JB thrives on structure and that's exactly what Year 1 is all about—more structure than play.

Unfortunately, this was where the problems really started. The subject of medication arose quickly in this year and I had to fight hard!

My story

A note about medication

When our journey with ADHD began, I didn't want to medicate my child at all. I fought against it. Even when we were trying to conceive, I told my husband that, if we had a child with ADHD, I would never medicate. I would try everything in my power first before going to medication. And I did.

But this doesn't mean I judge anyone for medicating their child. I know children whose lives have been transformed by it. Parents do what they need to do to discover what works for their children. My feeling is that medication isn't right for us as a family right now, but this could change going forward and it doesn't mean it isn't right for yours.

Life with ADHD is a journey, and each one is unique. But at least we have one thing in common—we all fight tooth and nail to do what's best for these beautiful children.

Beyond the ADHD Label
One Mother's Struggle for Change

So here we were in Year 1 and we were trying everything under the sun. Yet the school was asking us to consider medicating JB. But I wasn't willing to go there unless I had to.

Problems continued to escalate and we continually put different strategies in place to deal with them, but it didn't seem to be helping. The decision had to be made one way or another. So one day I took a lonely trip to the psychiatrist in tears, knowing I would leave her office with a script for the Ritalin I detested so much.

And that's what happened. I explained the situation and she felt we had no choices left. I took the script home and thought about it some more. My husband and I agreed to try the medication over the following weekend.

We spoke to JB about why we needed to try these tablets and he was OK with the decision. Then an unexpected problem arose—taking the tablets! JB hadn't taken tablets before, so he couldn't swallow them.

(Note: Some medications are OK to crush and some are not. Some you can mix with water. You may want to ask your doctor or pharmacist if there are other alternatives for you. A compounding pharmacy might put together a script for you

My story

and add a flavour that your child may like, making it easier for them to take.)

Once we finally got JB taking tablets (a battle in itself!), we increased the dosage until we found one that worked, which was great except that we also got the side effects. And what side effects we got! Insomnia, anxiety, sickness, headaches...we had the lot!

School became impossible—when I could actually get him there through the sickness and anxiety. And then the afternoons were worse. JB was either completely wild or overly emotional. No matter what we tried, we couldn't find a way to make it work. It was exhausting!

So, ultimately, we decided to dump the medication. Clearly his body was not ready for it. My husband and I did argue about this, as he knew I didn't want to medicate and thought I was looking for excuses to stop. But, honestly, if it had worked I would've put my tail between my legs and admitted defeat. But it hadn't worked and I was wrung out.

With the support of JB's psychiatrist, we decided to revisit the idea of medication in the future. For now, I had to find other options.

Beyond the ADHD Label
One Mother's Struggle for Change

(Read more about our journey with medication, including my raw journal entries of that time, later in the book.)

The ultimatum

Another term arrived and it brought yet another meeting with the school. This one was a doozy. They said they'd tried everything they could with JB and were out of options. They said we had to medicate or he would be put on 'managed attendance'—perhaps only a few hours a day.

I was furious! The school had been supportive for so long and now they said my child had to be medicated or his hours would be reduced. Once again, I was an emotional wreck. Our psychiatrist confirmed that medication wasn't the way to go at this time, so I started looking for alternative school options. I even considered home schooling, but couldn't see it working with my home business and his social challenges.

At the next school appointment, my husband and I stated that we would not medicate. Although they apologised for presenting me with what seemed an ultimatum, they did ultimately put JB on managed attendance, meaning he may be at school only two hours some days. (And I'm still trying to run my business around these hours today!)

My story

The first two weeks of managed attendance went well, as my husband was home on holidays and could do the running about. After that, it was a bit of a challenge. However, it didn't end up being two-hour days—just early afternoon pickups every few days—so that wasn't so bad.

I continued to think about schooling options for JB. In my heart, I knew that home schooling was my best option, but I also knew that running a busy home business and home schooling wouldn't work together. He just wouldn't get the teaching he needed.

I even considered getting a nanny, so I could home school for a while and then he could be looked after while I worked.

Of course, money was a limiting factor. We didn't have the money to afford many of these options—we generally live month to month—but I still needed to know *all* the options and then I could figure out how to get the money later. My philosophy is 'whatever has to be done has to be done'.

After much research, we decided to trial a different school system. After many appointments, we took JB for a trial at one of the schools. He lasted only five hours! It broke my heart to

Beyond the ADHD Label
One Mother's Struggle for Change

have to cross yet another option off the list. I'd like to say that a long-term solution finally presented itself but it hasn't yet.

JB stayed home with me for a while, which made it difficult to run a business, train staff and get him to do his school work. Then we got the call from the school to arrange another meeting and this time we were seriously looking at the two-hour days. Stress anyone? You might say that!

After many meetings with the school, we finally figured out ways for it to work for all of us. We felt that sending JB home on reduced days gave him the wrong message, so we pushed for him to stay at school all day. So the school developed another strategy where JB would finish his work in a higher year's classroom or in the office. This seemed to work for a while and, eventually, he moved back into the classroom for more time.

Today we still keep in contact with the school, and strategies range from consequences for behaviour to being sent to the office to finish his work. And they seem to be working for the moment. However, we all know that having a child living with ADHD means things can change in an instant. So we do the

My story

best we can with what we have in each moment and be ready to change when we need to.

(Read more about the various schooling options we investigated later in the book.)

Beyond the ADHD Label
One Mother's Struggle for Change

ADHD in society

Dealing with ignorance

ADHD is a normal part of society—people either accept that or they don't. And, trust me, many don't!

As a parent of a child with ADHD, you will often hear people say 'That kid just needs a good smack', 'You're too soft on them', 'ADHD doesn't exist, it's just an excuse for poor parenting' and even 'ADHD wasn't around when I was a kid, so why is it here now?'

Many of these comments come from people who are ignorant about what ADHD is. And I was one of these people many years ago. I believed ADHD was too frequently diagnosed and that some parents use it as an excuse for their child's bad behaviour.

I have since learned so much about ADHD that I don't think that way anymore.

Actually, I'll be honest—I *do* believe some parents use it as an excuse to not parent properly! But I'm also sure that, if you've

Beyond the ADHD Label
One Mother's Struggle for Change

picked up this book because you want to learn more about parenting a child living with ADHD, you're not this parent.

I always say: 'These kids are going to change the world—it's up to us to guide them correctly!' ADHD kids think entirely differently than we do. Just have a conversation about something they're interested in and you'll see how they think. It's so interesting!

As a parent of a child living with ADHD, you often feel like you're being judged on your child's behaviour. You're scared to tell people that your child lives with ADHD because you fear what they'll think of you. And you know they'll want to offer their opinion.

I've had several people in shopping centres voice their opinions on my son's behaviour, from 'You need to smack that child' to 'He is way too active for his own good'. Generally, I ignore these comments because it isn't their business why my child is like this. However, if they've really annoyed me, I tell them he lives with ADHD, and that the outside environment is becoming too much for him at this moment and this is what happens.

ADHD in society

If we don't put these people in their place and inform them about ADHD, one day they're going to say something to one exhausted and frustrated mum that will tip her over the edge. Society needs to be educated!

I believe you should tell as many people as you can about ADHD. This is the only way society is going to understand it, which will help people be more understanding.

Before I go into more detail about our journey with ADHD, there is one thing I'd love to see better understood in society: the difference between a tantrum and a meltdown.

Tantrum versus meltdown

Nothing annoys me more than hearing someone say a child is having a meltdown when they're actually just having a tantrum. The term 'meltdown' is so overused at the moment.

A few times, I've corrected people when they've said my son is having a meltdown, saying, 'No, he's throwing a tantrum'. It really isn't anyone's fault, as some people just don't understand the difference.

From my studies and various expert opinions that I've gathered, this is how I perceive the difference:

Beyond the ADHD Label
One Mother's Struggle for Change

A tantrum

A tantrum is usually associated with toddlers or small children. (Though, let's face it, some adults throw tantrums from time to time.)

A tantrum usually occurs when someone doesn't get something they want. It's usually driven by a desire or a goal.

When the tantrum is occurring, the person usually looks for acknowledgment that it's happening. This could be getting attention from another person, getting what they want out of the behaviour or even getting negative responses.

The behaviour that is a tantrum is likely to stop once the person receives what they want.

A meltdown

Like tantrums, a meltdown can happen at any age; however, it's often caused by a sensory overload. The person having it generally has no goals for the behaviour.

They don't look for attention when a meltdown is occurring and have no control over what they're doing. As a result, they may hurt themselves. If you're with a person having a meltdown, ensure they don't do this.

A meltdown may take some time to end, while a tantrum will usually end quickly.

If you parent a child who has meltdowns, you will learn to notice signs that may lead to a meltdown. This can help you prevent it. In comparison, a tantrum is quick to happen and there are few, if any, signs.

Similarities

Some people don't see the difference between a tantrum and a meltdown because both can involve screaming, kicking, shouting, stomping, swearing, biting, hitting, punching and even throwing things.

As parents, we need to take a step back and think about where the child's behaviour stemmed from. What do they want out of the behaviour? Are they looking for attention or not?

Beyond the ADHD Label
One Mother's Struggle for Change

The key point

When a true meltdown is occurring, it's extremely unlikely that you've done anything wrong, so you can't blame yourself. Your child is experiencing an overload and you can't help that.

The best way through it is to let them work out their emotions with your guidance and support.

A few stories spring to mind about some of JB's meltdowns and how I handled them at the time.

The day we went to school early

One morning, I was driving my son to school. I had prepared him the night before that we'd be going school early because I had a meeting to attend. Usually, we get to school just as the bell goes, so he doesn't have to deal with the chaos of children getting organised in the morning.

So, on this occasion, we did a lot of talking to help JB understand what would happen in the morning—first the night before and then on the way to school. He seemed OK with it.

ADHD in society

But then we arrived at the school car park and I told JB it was time to get out of the car. The reality hit him—it was time to get out of the car. He refused. I knew immediately what was about to happen and that he wouldn't be getting out of the car.

Gently, I reminded him that we'd spoken about the plan and this is what had to happen. He still refused. Panic started to set in—I had an important appointment and he really needed to get out of the car.

I felt myself getting angry, knowing I wouldn't be able to control this situation myself. I needed to stop and think. What could I do?

I decided to call the person I was meeting to advise that I'd be late, which bought me some time to deal with the situation at hand.

Then I tried to get JB out of the car. I think I used every parenting tactic in the book: anger, consequence, talking, explaining, ignoring…but nothing worked. He worked himself into such a meltdown mess that he ended up on the car floor screaming hysterically with no idea why he was screaming. Clearly, whatever I was doing wasn't working. I needed help.

Beyond the ADHD Label
One Mother's Struggle for Change

I'd parked near the school office, so I left JB in the car knowing he'd be safe and went to ask for help. That was the first time I'd asked someone for help with my son—and it was scary! Luckily, a teacher he liked came down and talked him out of the car.

I learned a lot from that situation. The big one was that I can't always do everything myself. Sometimes I need to ask someone for help. In that situation, nothing I'd done would have worked. His mind was telling him he should arrive at school *when* the bell goes, not *before*. He wouldn't accept anything else. All I could do was control as much as I could and then accept that everything else was out of my control.

As difficult as it sounds, if you can think of these things while trying to work through these meltdowns as rationally as possible, you may find yourself being calmer for it. But it does takes practice. I've spent more mornings than I care to admit crying in my car. But, like all daily practices, you will start to see small improvements until the habit becomes ingrained and you react this way automatically.

ADHD in society

The day we had too many children

On another occasion, my son experienced a meltdown due to a sensory overload from having too many children in our home at once. I tried to send him to his room to calm down and distance himself from the other children, but he didn't want that. He was very over-stimulated and I could see a meltdown brewing.

Gently, I told him he needed to stay in his room until he calmed down. He started screaming, hitting and throwing things around his room. I said, 'I know you're frustrated right now and that's OK. I'll stay in here to make sure you don't hurt yourself. And whatever you mess up in your bedroom, you'll have to clean up later.'

He continued to throw things around the room as I stood there and ignored him. Eventually, he calmed down. I let a little more time pass so the meltdown wouldn't brew again and then reminded him to tidy his room, which he did.

This incident showed me the benefit of staying calm. In this situation, there's no point increasing your stress levels because your child will feed off that and make a bad situation worse. Remind them of the consequences and ensure you follow through once they're calm.

There's no point trying to rationalise with them while they're heated; just let them be and work through it. It's very hard as a parent to remain calm while they're irrational and this is something to work on over time. I find myself getting very emotional at these times, but I try to control it and remind myself that it will pass. It takes practice and patience.

Afterwards, you should discuss what happened. Ask your child about their feelings leading up to the incident. Have them think about what caused it. They may not know and that's OK. Tell them to think about it throughout the day and you'll ask again later.

Talk to them about an alternative solution. When you understand their feelings leading up to the incident, you can ask them to consider other ways they could've handled it. Don't put words into their mouth; let them tell you. Their answer may surprise you.

A great book that I can recommend on this area is *The Explosive Child* by Dr Ross W Greene[4]. He has some great strategies you can try. Like me, you'll probably spend the first

ADHD in society

section of his book laughing, crying and nodding your head, thinking this book was written about *your* child.

For the rest of this book, I'm going to devote each chapter to an aspect of life with ADHD and how we've dealt with it—sometimes well, sometimes not! Hopefully you'll relate to some of it and even get some new ideas if you're currently struggling through it. Remember, you're not alone!

Beyond the ADHD Label
One Mother's Struggle for Change

Having friends (or not)

One of the hardest things I've found about raising a child with ADHD is losing my friends and not making any new ones. But, while this is hard for me, the hardest thing without a doubt is my own child not having friends.

Making friends when you have ADHD

Picture this: You're at the school helping at an event and you see children in the playground having a great time. Then you see a little boy sitting up against the building by himself watching the kids play. And you realise this is your own child. As you lock eyes with him, he runs over to you with so much emotion that he starts to cry. Heartbreaking, right?

If you're the parent of a child living with ADHD, this may be a common sight for you. It's certainly one that broke my heart. I will never get rid of that image of my little boy sitting by himself while other children played.

Sometimes it's really hard for these children to make friends because they can't control their impulses. They get angry quickly in a situation they don't understand, which can lead to

Beyond the ADHD Label
One Mother's Struggle for Change

hitting, kicking and punching. Or they may want to keep control of a situation so they can keep control of themselves—but other kids don't want to be controlled.

I've seen it over and over. No one wants to play with JB because he can't interact like the other kids or he just wants to be by himself on a particular day. This results in him not being invited to birthday parties or play dates.

As a parent, it takes you back to your own school days when someone didn't invite you to their party or ask you to play with them. You want to protect your own child from this pain.

You can only help your child through this by talking to them each day about other things they could do in their lunch break or help them find solutions for how they can play with others.

The effect on your friendships

Of course, your child's social problems may also reflect on you. People may not want to spend time with you unless they have to because your child and their child may have to play together—and they don't know how to deal with that.

Having friends (or not)

It would be easier if ADHD were more accepted and understood in society, as people would be more understanding and talk to their children about it.

So, unfortunately, you should be prepared to lose friends. Some will see you as a bad parent and lose respect for you, so your friendships will start to fade. Others will fade away because you're just too busy to meet them for coffee or dinner dates.

Sometimes you won't like how some friends relate to your child, so you'll start stepping away from them yourself. And others will have children who don't get along with your child, so it isn't worth the time and effort to keep the friendship.

Sometimes you'll find out that your child is considered 'the naughty one' among your friends' children. Be prepared! Your child may be blamed for just about everything, which will take a toll on you with all the dobbing, fighting and whinging from the kids.

Beyond the ADHD Label
One Mother's Struggle for Change

The good news

Hey, it's not all bad. Quickly, you'll find out who your real friends are—the ones you can depend on when you most need them. They'll understand your child and their little quirks, and try their best to manage them. They'll come and sit with you when you need it and maybe bring a bottle of wine with them! They'll be there to help you talk though the hardest decisions you need to make for your child. They'll just be there for you.

So even though sometimes you may feel like throwing it all in and not socialising anymore, stick with it! Our kids need to socialise, so talk to your friends about how you're feeling. Ask them to explain to their children that your child thinks differently than they do and that they should accept it so everyone can play nicely.

It's all about preparation. The more we can prepare ourselves, our children, our friends and our friends' children, the smoother the process will be—and the less stress you'll need to endure just for a play date.

Having friends (or not)

Put your children into as many social situations as possible so they learn to socialise effectively. Be nearby as much as you can to guide them while still letting them learn their own way. This will prepare them for the many social situations they'll face in their lifetime.

Also, by talking to all your friends about ADHD, you'll be doing your part to make it more acceptable in the community. The more that people accept and understand ADHD rather than stay ignorant about it, the better our children will be embraced.

Beyond the ADHD Label
One Mother's Struggle for Change

ADHD and your relationship

We all know that having children can change the dynamic of a marriage or partnership for better *and* for worse. Having a child who lives with ADHD is no exception and can add a great deal of pressure to the relationship if you let it.

In a relationship, it's not unusual for the responsibility for appointments and child support to fall more to one parent than the other. This can bring enormous stress and resentment as one parent has to deal with the 'drama' every day. It can get really tiring.

I remember back in the day care period that I was picking up JB every afternoon, so I was the one getting daily reports from teachers about his behaviour. It was draining to be told almost every day that my son wasn't complying. I felt so overwhelmed with this burden that I didn't know what to do. I did talk to my husband about it, but he didn't seem to get it because he wasn't experiencing it every day.

Eventually circumstances changed and my work hours increased, so my husband picked up JB twice a week. After a few weeks, he said to me, 'I hate picking up JB from day care. They always tell me how bad he's been. It's embarrassing'. Yeah, no kidding! I finally felt that he understood how I was feeling.

Having a child living with ADHD puts extra pressure on a relationship. I know of families that have broken up over it. Below are a few areas where you may disagree with your partner and some ideas for working together to resolve them.

Accepting the diagnosis

This may be one of your first disagreements regarding ADHD. One of you may not agree there is even such a thing as ADHD. This is a difficult diagnosis to accept. ADHD has such a stigma about it that, deep down, you or your partner may not want to believe it exists or tell people your child lives with ADHD.

All I can say here is be gentle. This is a mindset that will be very hard to work with and change. If you are ready to accept the diagnosis, understand that your partner may need more time. If this is the case, take your partner to as many appointments as possible. Find them some great videos or articles on ADHD or, if they won't speak about it, leave the information lying around and they may just pick it up. Share articles on Facebook and they may decide to open one.

You can only take small steps with this; eventually, they may come around. Of course, in the meantime, you may be left to cope with school, day care, changes in house routine and anything else that needs to be done. Be patient. Once your partner starts accepting and understanding ADHD better, life will get easier. It may even be an outside person who says something to them and it finally clicks.

Parenting styles

Different parenting styles can cause friction in whatever family arrangement you have and it's something you may always need to work on.

Mothers generally have more emotional responses in their parenting style. They often have more patience and exhibit nurturing behaviour. Historically, men were raised to be protectors and the 'hunters' for the family. Their job was to protect the family at all costs. As a result, even today, they can come across as stern and generally deal with the child's behaviour less emotionally.

Beyond the ADHD Label
One Mother's Struggle for Change

My husband and I actually have very similar backgrounds, which we have both grown out of and learned from. However, we are also 15 years apart, which means we've brought some very different parenting styles to the relationship. My husband has three grown children from a previous marriage who were parented in a way that suited the time. My parenting style is completely different and the specialists used to challenge us on this. They wanted us to be on the same page for consistency but we definitely were not.

Ultimately, my husband and I agreed that neither of us was going to change our parenting style, despite who may be 'right' or 'wrong', so we all had to learn to work with these differences.

We discussed what was working and developed a parenting strategy around that. I can tell you it wasn't (and sometimes still isn't) smooth sailing, but we are getting there and things are starting to settle down.

It's usually best to avoid trying to change your partner's parenting style. I'd suggest focusing on what does work for both of you and work with that. You won't agree all the time — that's just parenting in general — but focus on what you do agree about and build from there. Life with a child living with ADHD is already so much work without constant arguments about parenting styles.

We all love our children and will do anything for them; we just have different ways of showing it and dealing with the situations our children put us in.

Disciplinary action

Disciplinary action could also fall under parenting styles. Parents of children living with ADHD often disagree on the most appropriate disciplinary action to enforce. One may feel that whatever the child did couldn't be helped as the ADHD took over. In this case, giving the child a talking-to may seem more appropriate than laying down a harsh consequence. However, the other parent may feel a harsh consequence is needed.

This is a tough situation. In our house, we don't allow excuses due to ADHD because JB still needs to learn right and wrong. However, as I've learned more about ADHD, I've started to understand his world, and what he can and can't control. This helps me decide whether something needs a harsh consequence or not. However, my husband hasn't done as much reading on ADHD and, as mentioned above, he has a different parenting style. So sometimes he pushes for the harsher consequence.

In these situations, I've learned that sometimes I just have to run with it. This is my husband's reality at the time, not mine, and we have to deal with each situation as it arises. If I feel strongly that a consequence isn't necessary, we'll discuss it (away from JB) and work out a consequence that we might agree on next time. Sometimes it works and sometimes it doesn't, but ultimately clear communication is key.

A meltdown or a tantrum

Earlier in the book, I discussed meltdowns versus tantrums and this is an area that you and your partner may disagree on. A meltdown is a sensory overload not a rebellious dummy spit, so no amount of yelling and screaming is going to make it better. If you or your partner try to discipline a meltdown, it will create even more friction in the household and, importantly, it won't work.

The important thing is that you both understand the difference between the two so you can deal with it appropriately. Use the correct terminology yourself and research some information on how best to deal with these situations (starting with my chapter earlier in the book).

Naughty behaviour versus ADHD symptoms

Many parents make excuses for their child because they live with ADHD and this often causes tension in their relationship.

As I mentioned earlier, my husband and I agree that, although JB lives with ADHD, he can't get away with hitting, kicking, punching or yelling at someone—this must be dealt with. When parents start using ADHD as an excuse for bad behaviour, they're giving their child permission to behave this way.

Treatment options

As there are now many treatment options for children living with ADHD, one parent may be open to trying different things while another may not. I can relate to this, as I'm an alternative thinker and can sometimes be pretty out there.

Beyond the ADHD Label
One Mother's Struggle for Change

After 22 years together, I think my husband has learned to just 'put up with' all the new things I want to try—and if they work, it's a bonus!

If you do want to try something different, discuss it with your partner. Explain that trying new things can't hurt and, if they don't work, you can admit defeat and move on. We've tried many things that haven't worked, but then found that things we thought wouldn't work actually helped a bit. So you never know until you try.

You may need to do a lot of research and present the facts if you have a partner who likes to know everything beforehand. There's nothing wrong with being like that, so if it's what you need to do, then do it. Help them understand exactly what you're going to do and why.

Schooling options

Schooling options can be challenging even in a family that doesn't have special needs, such as the debate on state schools versus private schools. When choosing a school for your child living with ADHD, again do your research. Make appointments with the schools and ask lots of questions. Where possible, ensure both parents attend the school

ADHD and your relationship

meeting and ask all your questions while you're there—whether or not you think your partner will agree with those questions.

When I wanted to trial the Montessori system, I thought there was no way my husband would agree. He loved the school we already had, as his other three children had gone there as well. So he was emotionally attached.

When Montessori had an open day, I told him I was going. I'd already been to the Steiner school open day and hadn't been able to get him to that. However, I did feel that Montessori would be a great option for us, so I asked him straight out if he would come. I told him it would mean a lot to me if he'd see what it was about. He agreed but maintained that he wasn't interested in moving our son at all. I accepted his feelings but was glad he was coming with me.

Sometimes you have to take the little wins and find something that works for both of you. If your partner is reticent, talk it through, voice your concerns and ask them to just humour you and see how it goes. As with all relationship issues, there needs to be give and take on both sides.

Medication options

The subject of medicating children can cause a massive problem in relationships. One parent may be all for medication and the other completely against it. So, for this issue, you may need to seek help from a professional, as you will both have reasons why you will or won't trial or accept medication— possibly strong and emotional ones.

In the end, the medical professional may be the one who tells you it must be done. Either way, it is essential that parents respect each other's concerns regarding medication and ultimately do what's right for the child.

Shared responsibility

When you have a child living with ADHD, there are always appointments to attend. Unfortunately, due to different working conditions, one parent often ends up taking responsibility for most of the appointments. This can take a huge toll on the relationship.

If you are this parent, it can be a hard road. Not only are you juggling other work or home commitments around the appointments, but you're relaying all the information to the specialists and hearing all the feedback on treatments and strategies your child needs. Then you may feel that the burden is on you to implement it all.

Sometimes it can all get too much. If this happens, you may need to ask your partner to attend appointments with you to share the feedback or even attend some of the appointments themselves.

For example, you might try booking appointments after hours so you can take turns to share the appointment duties. Work out a schedule so everyone knows what everyone is doing.

What's important is that one parent isn't getting overwhelmed, as supporting a child with ADHD can be time consuming but also take an emotional toll.

Other children

Having a child living with ADHD can have a huge effect on other children in the house. Sometimes they may feel excluded, resentful towards their sibling living with ADHD and resentful towards you for giving their sibling too much attention.

Beyond the ADHD Label
One Mother's Struggle for Change

The household may be in turmoil due to the pressures of ADHD, which could cause problems between you and your partner. And the other children may start developing their own problems as well.

It can be hard to juggle the needs of everyone in the house and you can only do your best.

Parents with these issues have told me they try to get regular one-on-one time with each child so they feel they're getting equal attention. Even if it's just to the shops or out for a walk, any activity that gives them one-on-one time is great. They also help the children understand the needs of someone living with ADHD, so they understand the way their sibling thinks (though it's more difficult with very young children).

You may be able to enlist grandparents, aunties, uncles and friends to babysit while you enjoy time together. They might even take the siblings out for some one-on-one time themselves.

A child who has special needs will always take more time from you than a child who doesn't. It takes time to perfect the art of balancing family time. But, while you do, you'll get to enjoy lots of great family time together and create lasting memories.

Summary

Parenting creates challenges in a marriage or partnership at the best of times and the key to success is always open communication. Sometimes I struggle to comprehend how we can talk so openly with our best friends but find it hard to talk openly with the partner that we get into bed with every night. It's definitely something we all need to work on every day.

Sometimes we assume our partner's response before they give it. How fair is that for us to become defensive before we've even asked the question?

In my efforts to maintain a solid marriage while parenting a child living with ADHD, I've learned the following things:

- Try to keep an open mind and accept whatever your partner is going to say, but don't assume you know what it is beforehand.

- Try to talk rationally about things that are important to you. Tell your partner how you're feeling and don't blame them for making you feel this way. You are the only one who can allow someone to make you feel something. Put your feelings and thoughts on the table and let them see your point of view.
- Start looking at the good side of ADHD and incorporate it into your household. My section on mindset later in the book should give you some great tips for thinking a different way about ADHD and bringing more positivity into your life.
- Never be afraid to get help with your relationship. You and your partner loved each other enough to have a child together, so why not try everything to make it work. See a counsellor if you need to. It's nothing to be ashamed of and can really help if you need strategies for negotiating the types of issues I've discussed above.

It takes time but you will get there. I am not saying it will be perfect by any means. You'll still have your hard times when issues escalate again and you and your partner strongly

ADHD and your relationship

disagree. But every mountain you climb together can make you stronger.

Of course, there is no shame in leaving a relationship that is past the point of repair. If you have reached a point of unhappiness that can't be fixed, you need to look after yourself.

No matter what, you need to be strong to parent a child living with ADHD—and you've come this far, so you know you're strong enough. Look after yourself first and your whole family will be better for it.

Beyond the ADHD Label
One Mother's Struggle for Change

To medicate or not medicate

I briefly touched on this topic earlier in this book when I told you my story, but now I want to dive into it a little deeper. Over the course of writing this book, things changed regarding medication and I kept a journal as it all happened. Just reading it again takes me right back there and hurts my heart.

I'm going to let you read these journal entries now. This is a very personal story but, hopefully, you might see some of your own story in it too.

Trust me when I say that, whether you medicate your child or not, this is not an easy path. You'll be judged if you do and if you don't.

And let me be clear: As I stated earlier in the book, I'm not here to tell you to medicate or not medicate. I believe medication has its place and only you as a parent can make that choice. You can't take on everyone else's opinions about this. (And everyone has one!) The best you can do is listen to experts but then trust your gut instinct and make the right decision for you.

The decision I made may not be for you or may not be a decision that needs to be made right now. This is my journey, and yours is your own.

24th February 2015 - Resisting the medication (the 'M' word)

All medication comes with pros and cons. Deciding whether to medicate a child living with ADHD is such a hard decision and one that can make you feel very alone.

For example, even as I write this, today has NOT been a good day for me.

JB had a psychiatrist appointment this afternoon and I spent the hour-long car trip in and out of tears.

I knew what was coming.

I've been fighting it for years.

It was inevitable.

Medication!

Anyone who knows me knows how hard I've fought this battle for my six-year-old son to not be medicated for his condition.

To medicate or not medicate

Since he was expelled from day care at the age of four, I've resisted the comments and opinions about having him medicated. We've been told he has ADHD, ASD, ODD, anxiety…but who really knows? This is the problem—no one does! So what exactly are we medicating for???

When he started school last year, the medication discussion was taken seriously, but I refused. I thought he might respond to structure better when he reached Year 1. We agreed to wait until the end of Term 1 and make a decision in the second term. I was still not 100 per cent on board with medication but I was willing to consider it with a little time on my side.

But that time is up now!

JB is not handling the structure - in fact he's worse and not finishing his work. We're lucky that he's very bright and ahead of the curriculum in lots of subjects, but we won't have that luxury forever.

The school has asked us to consider this early. Which brings me to today and our psychiatrist visit.

After everything we've tried, this seems to be our last hope. I left my full-time job to build a business, so I do have the time to give to him by supporting his school activities, attending school excursions so he can attend, have ongoing meetings with the school to ensure we're all on the same page, picking him up from school when he can't handle a full day and running him to numerous appointments.

We've done the diet, a special school pre-prep program, a private special needs teacher, a psychologist, a paediatrician, an occupational therapist, essential oils, a positive parenting program (twice!), behavioural management, natural therapies, hearing checks, grommets in and adenoids out...

We've officially tried it all!

So why do I feel like I've been defeated because I'm getting a script for medication?

I now believe that our only chance is medication and, if that fails, home schooling. But we're so hard on ourselves as mums, and the way we beat ourselves up with these decisions is crazy. If JB needed lifesaving medication or glasses to see better or hearing aids to hear better, I wouldn't think twice. So why is this so hard?

I don't know.

To medicate or not medicate

Well, I have the script and a meeting with the school next week to discuss our next step. A little piece of me has died just by agreeing to the script - it might actually kill me to physically give him this medication.

Stay tuned and I'll update you when we start the medication (if I can actually do it) and on how it all goes.

28th February 2015 - The medication decision

Well today was the day. We've made the decision - the medication has entered the house!

But I couldn't do it myself. I literally couldn't make myself go to the chemist and get the script filled - it was just too heartbreaking. My husband did it and the pills are now in our house.

I kept it together enough to tell JB why he was taking the tablets. We told him as little as possible, only that we're trying the tablets to see if they help him sit still at school. He very sweetly said, 'Will they help me stay at my desk?' That was the killer question and I heard my voice waver as I said, 'Hopefully they will, honey.'

Beyond the ADHD Label
One Mother's Struggle for Change

He's obviously aware of it - he's not dumb. He knows he's different. He knows that his brain makes him do things he can't control (his words, not mine).

At the school meeting, we were greeted by the learning support teacher, the Year 1 teacher and the guidance counsellor. I walked in the room and immediately looked for the tissues, just in case.

Despite my husband telling me he was just going to march in there and tell them they can't demand we put JB on medication, he was actually very civil. Phew, one less stress!

In truth, they didn't demand it at all. They told us the problems: he can't sit still; he spends more time under the desk than at it; he's losing friends, as he isn't very nice and is quite bossy; they're struggling to find things to praise him for, etc. We're really worried about his mental health and how all this will affect what he thinks of himself.

After 20 years of work to get my own self-confidence back, I certainly don't want my son having this long battle either.

To medicate or not medicate

So, although I feel like I have no choice in doing this, we do have to give it a go. I'm trying to look at it as just another option that we're trying among a massive list of other things.

It might not even work, who knows! (But then what??)

So Saturday is the day. Not sure if I'm actually going to be able to give it to him, but we'll see.

7th March 2015 - This medication is killing ME!

Saturday arrived and so did the medication.

We'd prepped JB that it was happening and told him it would be Saturday, but he had to have breakfast first. Then we were ready to go...well, as ready as we could be.

To start with, it definitely wasn't all fun and games. He had to be convinced to take the tablet. This was SO hard.

JB hadn't taken tablets before, so he couldn't swallow them. It was quite a scene. My sometimes hot-headed husband was yelling at JB that he had to take the tablet, while I tried the gently-gently approach and then had to leave the room in tears after watching him struggle to take it.

Beyond the ADHD Label
One Mother's Struggle for Change

Finally, I sent my husband away and quietly convinced JB to take the tablet. Now we just needed to wait for the effect...or not!

Yep, nothing—no changes, no side effects. The biggest side effect we got was the battle to take the tablets.

JB asked if we could call his brother to talk about taking tablets (as his brother is 31 and was medicated as a child). JB asked his brother if he was scared when he took his tablets. A little part of my heart just died, knowing he was scared of doing this.

After a few more days, we still had no change so we increased the dose.

Then the side effects arrived. Wow, did they arrive—insomnia, anxiety, sickness headaches...

We actually think it's the stress of taking the tablets combined with the actual side effects to the tablet. He can't sleep until late at night, as he's literally buzzing, then he gets up in the morning panicked that he has to take his tablet. Then he feels sick from the tablet by the time he gets to school and he's got a cold on top of it all.

To medicate or not medicate

With all that, his anxiety levels have escalated and, for the last two days, I haven't even got him to his classroom! This morning, he got halfway there and got hold of a pole in the school yard and wouldn't let go.

Oh my God...talk about stress! Afterwards, I was a blubbering mess in the car.

This is crazy! Asking me to medicate my child when I have to watch him go through all these things on top of not wanting to do it! I'm not sure I can do this.

So today, as well as trying to run a business, I was on the phone and email with his psychiatrist and the school guidance counsellor trying to work out what we can do.

I've also been researching yet another path we can consider if we can't do the medication. We have until mid this week to work out whether we're going to continue with this path at this stage.

Part of me just wants to give up and take the medication away, and the other part wishes it would just work so I can help him stop feeling this way. Not sure what we'll end up doing.

Beyond the ADHD Label
One Mother's Struggle for Change

5th April 2015 - Will the medication continue?

So, when I last left you, I wrote about the dramas of the medication and JB's (and my!) heightened anxiety around this.

Well, not much has changed. In fact, in some ways it's worse!

After talking with the school, we worked out a strategy that seemed to remove the anxiety around actually taking the tablet and the build-up we had in the morning getting JB to the classroom (i.e. he would go to the office with a favourite teacher and take the tablet with her). First challenge down!

But (a huge but!) my afternoons are an absolute disaster! The minute I pick him up from school, he's on a high!

He's on short-acting medication, which means the meds should be out of his system by lunch time and the school should be getting the high, not me. They definitely notice the difference when the medication wears off but, for some reason, I get the worst of it and no one can work out why.

As soon as I pick him up, he goes wild, impulsively running in front of cars (which he has NEVER done before; he's always held my hand but now refuses to), jumping in the boot of my

To medicate or not medicate

car as soon as I open it and then jumping in the back seat and getting up on the parcel tray of the car.

We're fighting before we're even out of the car park! And I can forget going to the shops now, that's just out of the question.

Most of this behaviour was rare before the medication.

Then, if we don't have more wild behaviour in the afternoon, we have an extremely emotional child who falls to pieces at the mere whisper of 'No'.

I'm getting kicked, punched and yelled at by a six year old and I'm a mess by the time my husband gets home. He has to take over, as I'm done!

Then, to top it off, JB doesn't go to sleep until 9.30–10pm at night!

The other day I actually locked myself in a parents' room at a shopping centre and called a girlfriend to stop me falling apart, as he was being wild and I couldn't get him back in the car.

It just doesn't make sense to anyone—his teachers, us, his specialists. They all say this shouldn't be happening, as the meds should be out of his system well and truly. But it most certainly is happening!

His psychologist and I agree this is no good for him. For the few hours that the school is getting results, it's affecting the rest of his day negatively, especially our relationship.

So, with help from his psychiatrist, we've decided we won't do the meds at all over the upcoming school holidays and see how he goes. Then we'll send him back to school with no meds and see what happens.

Meanwhile, I'm planning to meet with yet another specialist who has many qualifications in a lot of natural therapies and a psychology degree. And I'm currently doing a course on ADHD and ASD and reading a book written by a psychologist about various treatments to try. Hopefully some of it will help!

4th June 2015 - The decision making continues

Well, it seems sometimes good things really do come to an end.

When I last wrote, I spoke about how the medication escalated JB's behaviour in the afternoon and he didn't sleep. So we took him off it for the school holidays and the first few weeks of school.

To medicate or not medicate

But now we've been called in for another meeting with the school and we're back at the beginning again! We've just been told that we're now looking at 'managed attendance', which means only 2–3 hours of school a day! It all depends how he's handling things on the day.

Now what do we do? Who knows!!!! I can imagine fun times ahead trying to run a business around that schooling schedule!

Once again, my head is in turmoil trying to decide what the best thing to do is! I feel like everyone except my own mum is backing me into a corner to medicate my son or he can't go to school like a normal kid!

We do have the option of another drug, which would be a full-time commitment of two months on our part to confirm whether or not it works. However, the side effects of this drug are enormous and I'm not comfortable with that at all!

So right now our options are very limited: find a school that can give him the help he needs and cater to his needs; medicate him with the possibility that it may not work; or home-school him.

Beyond the ADHD Label
One Mother's Struggle for Change

Really, running a business while home-schooling him isn't an option right now. But if that ends up being our only option, then I'll have to make it work.

We're definitely not ready to try medication again. None of us is in the right head space for medicating and dealing with the side effects for two months if they're anything like our last trial.

So now we're trying the managed attendance and I'm working that around my business as best I can. I'm working on lesson plans and have bought a heap of scholar books for him to work through when he comes home. I'm also interviewing for an assistant, which should help on the business side of things.

We're also trying a natural therapist who has made JB's already restricted diet gluten and dairy free. I've changed my own diet to be the same, so I can see if it affects me in any positive way as well. Given the number of products that have a gluten-free option now, I don't find this too hard, but dairy free is quite a challenge!

I've also decided that I need to meet other parents who are going through similar challenges with their children, so I've started looking for a support group. (Obviously I can't do this on my own anymore!)

To medicate or not medicate

Did you know there are no physical support groups for parents dealing with ADHD children?? There's plenty for ASD but not ADHD. This is huge! There are some on Facebook but nothing face to face.

So what am I going to do about that? Start my own, of course!

_____

So what now?

Our journey with medication has come to a stop for the moment. We won't be trialling any further. We haven't discounted it completely, and may consider it later in life, but right now we don't feel it's the right thing for him.

You may be dealing with this issue yourself. When you come to a crossroads in any form of treatment, not just medication, the best you can do is research everything until you're comfortable with your decision. Then stand by it.

There's definitely no right or wrong way with this and even the specialists can disagree. A mother's instinct is strong, so do what you feel is right because it's probably the best decision for your child.

And definitely join a supportive network of people, whether it be on Facebook or face to face. Don't let them judge you for whatever decision you make—and chances are they won't because they've been in the same position at least once before.

But you will be judged when it comes to medication.

So be prepared! No matter which way you go, whether you medicate or don't, you will be judged.

If you choose to medicate, not many people will understand the process you went through to make that decision. No parent wants to constantly medicate their child, no matter what it's for. But sometimes this is the best thing for the child.

Some people may believe that medicating your child is the easy way out and you just don't want to deal with your child. Of course, we know this isn't true.

If you don't medicate, people will ask you why. If you don't have the right specialists, they'll keep telling you that you need to medicate. If you don't have the right school support, they'll keep asking you to medicate your child.

The choice is yours, so stay strong with whatever you choose!

Choosing not to medicate

From experience, I can tell you that choosing not to medicate is something you need to be dedicated to. You'll need to source other therapies, such as intense occupational therapy, animal therapy, school therapies and strategies, and anything else you can get your hands on.

You'll need to be prepared to be challenged by your child constantly. One week, your strategies may work beautifully, and the next week they may not, forcing you to implement new strategies.

And then there are the really off-the-rail days! You will go from having a polite, quiet child playing with their toys to a child who is literally bouncing off the walls and throwing objects around his bedroom.

Have strategies in place to help them through the meltdowns (see my earlier section on tantrums versus meltdowns) and be prepared to drop everything in an instant to implement those strategies. If you don't, things will go from bad to worse in seconds.

Of course, all this can still happen with medication, but just be sure you have the strategies ready.

Beyond the ADHD Label
One Mother's Struggle for Change

The food question

When I tell people my son has ADHD, often the first question they ask is, 'Have you tried cutting out sugar? It's probably just sugar.'

Commonly, we also get, 'Have you tried a gluten-free diet?' Why yes I have and, actually, it just excluded my son even more for very little effect!

Our journey with food has been almost as interesting and, at times, stressful as that with medication, so it's worth telling you about our experience to give you some idea of what you may be in for if you go this way.

Eliminating numbers

Before we got our dietician—whom we chose because we wanted to do the Failsafe Elimination Diet—we decided to eliminate all numbers and preservatives. This is an easy way to see if you get any response.

Some people see a massive difference in their child's behaviour just doing this alone. And making different food choices may be all you need to reduce (not cure) outbursts or control them a little better.

There's a great app called The Chemical Maze³ that will help you enormously if you decide to do this. While you're in the supermarket, you just enter the numbers of a product that you normally purchase and the app tells you whether it may cause behavioural problems (among other things). For around $10, it's really useful.

However, although we did see a small change and still avoid some preservatives to this day, I wanted more.

Our failsafe journey

Basically, failsafe stands for 'free of additives, low in salicylates, amines and flavour enhancers'. It's a term coined by Sue Dengate in her book, *Fed Up*[5], for a low-chemical exclusion diet. Under the diet, you replace problem foods with healthy, low-chemical alternatives.

We decided to start our failsafe journey on 1 January 2013. Crazily, I decided to do the diet with my son and included no sugar for myself as well! With help from the dietician and Sue's

The food question

book, we stripped our diets back to bare basics. There was so much to learn. There were absolutely no processed foods and everything had to be cooked from scratch—and I mean everything!

We also eliminated all cleaning chemicals from the house. As I have extremely sensitive skin, I was happy to do that and there wasn't much in the house that I could use anyway.

I quickly learned about salicylates and amines, and how they can affect behaviour, skin conditions and other out-of-the-ordinary bodily functions.

Salicylates: A family of plant chemicals found naturally in many fruits, vegetables, nuts, herbs, spices, jams, honey, yeast extracts, tea, coffee, juices, beer, wine, flavourings, perfumes, scented toiletries and some medications.

Amines: From protein breakdown or fermentation. Large amounts are found in cheese chocolate, wine, beer, yeast extracts (bread), fish products, non-fresh meat, bananas, avocados and tomatoes.

As you can see, removing these from the diet doesn't leave much! We struggled particularly with the limited fruit and

Beyond the ADHD Label
One Mother's Struggle for Change

vegetables, as JB was an enthusiastic fruit and vegetable eater, but I knew it wouldn't be forever.

We had to continue this basic diet until our dietician was happy with our behaviour diary. The diary recorded the food JB had eaten throughout the day and any behaviour that had occurred. I provided all food to our day care with strict instructions that he eat nothing else and asked them to monitor his behaviour.

Our dietician was fairly confident that JB was an 'amine responder' due to his aggressive behaviour. (Amines can cause aggressive behaviour, while salicylates can cause depressive behaviour.)

Based on this, the dietician had us reintroduce fruits and vegetables that didn't contain amines to see if JB had a reaction. I was relieved to bring them back and very relieved when there was absolutely no response. He had passed the salicylates test!

The dietician was happy with this and decided JB could try the amines test. She warned me to brace for a response and we got one!

The food question

As bananas are extremely high in amines and JB loves bananas, we overloaded him with them, allowing him three per day. We also switched to supermarket bread, rather than bakery bread, as it's full of amines and preservatives. We held back the chocolate, as we wanted to see whether he responded to these foods first.

Day one was pretty good and we didn't really get a response.

Day two saw the behaviour start to escalate but nothing out of the ordinary.

Day three arrived and the amines kicked in loud and clear!

I was at my work desk when the receptionist called saying, 'I have your son's day care on the phone'. (We all know *that* phone call!) They said JB had had a reaction. I asked how bad—and it was bad. He'd kicked a teacher, bitten a child, smashed a computer, and been extremely non-compliant and unmanageable. I called the dietician in a panic and she told me to stop the bananas immediately. We'd found the culprit!

At our next meeting, she explained that taking three days to respond meant he was a slow amine responder. This meant he could still eat these foods if he was very heavily monitored and didn't eat them for days in a row, as they would build up and cause a reaction.

Finally, we had something we could control. As I said earlier, this certainly didn't cure anything, but knowing which foods set him off did help us.

We now eat only bakery-bought bread and heavily monitor anything with amines in it. Today JB is really good with his diet—considering he's been doing it for four years. He knows what he can and can't have, and we've taught him to identify how he's feeling with certain foods and let him make the choice. He usually makes a good choice. Like all kids, sometimes he doesn't, but I can't complain given his age.

The most important thing we can do is help JB relate the way he's feeling to any foods that may have caused it. By teaching him this, I hope he'll be able to make sensible food choices as he gets older.

Gluten and dairy free

This is another option that I hear people say has helped them. We did try gluten and dairy free under the guidance of a naturopath. We actually didn't see any changes at all with this elimination—in fact, we saw the behaviour worsen.

The food question

However, I have a theory that the behaviour worsened, not because of the food elimination, but because the diet excluded him from his peers even further. He already gets excluded in the classroom because he's 'different' from other children and therefore 'handled' differently in class. Then he can't join in and eat the same foods as his classmates.

He didn't feel like he was part of the group at school. If they had a celebration, he couldn't eat anything on the table. He had to sit down and eat the food I'd provided for him.

We decided this type of diet wasn't worth the exclusion that was making him sad. Given we saw no change, it wasn't worth excluding him further.

When deciding to try something new in this area, it's important to weigh up how it will affect your child. They're already battling to be 'normal', so you don't want to add to the battle by implementing diets or options that don't have a big impact but do affect their lives or self-esteem negatively.

Beyond the ADHD Label
One Mother's Struggle for Change

Now, if JB does attend school events where they have food, such as Christmas parties, we simply remind him to make good choices and leave the decision to him. We accept that, if he doesn't make the best choices, we'll just deal with the consequences.

We should all be thankful that our children's lives don't depend on them following a diet exactly and that, if they do go 'off' the diet and eat things that set them off, we just suffer the behaviour for a little bit.

And if your child's life does actually depend on them making strict diet choices when you're not around, I take my hat off to you! It would be so scary to allow your child freedom if they were anaphylactic and chose to eat something that had nuts in it.

School issues

The problem in Australia

Currently, in Australia, there's no funding in schools for children living with ADHD unless it's linked to something like autism, as they may get funding on the ASD banner. This needs to change! Children living with ADHD need as much support as children on the spectrum.

Having no funding puts enormous pressure on teachers. They can become stressed and under-resourced as they try to manage their time to assist a child living with ADHD in their classroom. As a result, the other children receive less attention. Alternatively, the child living with ADHD could become 'too hard' in the classroom and could be overlooked without the suitable resources.

This subject is a personal passion of mine. We should be jumping up and down to get help for these children. Yes, they can be a big disruption in the classroom, but how is discriminating against them going to help them get a fair education?

Beyond the ADHD Label
One Mother's Struggle for Change

If they're constantly asked to leave the classroom due to a behaviour they can't control, what will that do for their self-esteem? Chances are they already feel excluded because no one will play with them, they don't get invited to birthday parties and they're often excluded from school activities in general. Then their teacher deals with a behaviour they can't control by sending them out of the classroom. How are they understanding all this?

This lack of funding for schools means that you must be your child's constant advocate. You need to get heavily involved with the school, have regular meetings and ask the hard questions about what they're doing to help your child. Without funding, the help for children living with ADHD will be limited.

The two main issues are the lack of funding that schools receive for these children and the lack of training for teachers on how to 'deal' with them. Because of these issues, if children don't fit the mould of school and its curriculum, some teachers struggle. Teachers already have so much to juggle with the curriculum and meeting every child's needs that they must

School issues

have more support. It's not the fault of any one school or teacher—the system is letting them down.

We need to examine and learn from other countries' school systems where resources are in place for these children. For example, Finnish schools seem to be heading in the right direction, as they have various strategies that support children living with ADHD. Their children start school at a later age; they provide lots of movement breaks regardless of the weather; and their curriculum provides the opportunity for this freedom and flexibility.

Australia has a long way to go in this space. So, until things improve, we must be advocates for our children to ensure they receive the education they're entitled to.

Individual education plans (IEPs)

As a parent of a special needs child, you quickly learn about IEPs: individual education plans.

In Australia (and America as well), many schools use IEPs for some special needs students to enable parents and teachers to work as a team. These plans keep track of a child's performance in school, and determine their schooling needs and how they learn.

Beyond the ADHD Label
One Mother's Struggle for Change

Schools have used IEPs to:

- discuss the best way for the curriculum to work for the child
- adjust to a teaching style that will work with the child's learning needs
- create individual learning goals so the teacher and child can work together to meet their educational needs.

When your child first starts school or starts having problems, the school should talk to you about starting an IEP. You will have regular meetings with the school to go through your IEP, ensure standards are being met and set new goals. You will also discuss any curriculum changes where needed.

If you feel the curriculum doesn't suit your child or changes should be made, these meetings are a great chance to discuss that with the teachers. Allow enough time to go through it carefully.

You should take someone with you to the meetings to take notes. At least make sure they email a copy of the IEP to you after the meeting. If you're allowed to, record the meeting if you can't take notes.

School issues

The important thing is that you completely understand what's going to be done for your child to ensure their school experience is a great one.

This is an opportunity to see how the curriculum is working with your child. However, the school usually schedules this time to go through the IEP only. So if you have other issues outside the IEP, you should make another appointment, as this generally isn't the time for it.

Alternatively, if your time is limited, you could contact the school and ask for extra time to speak about concerns outside the IEP.

Our experience so far

We are extremely lucky with our school, as we've established a fantastic relationship with them and kept communication open on both sides. It's been a lot of work by both parties to get to this point, but we're in a nice place so far.

A big reason for this is that we were honest with them from the start. We advised them that JB had been asked to leave a day care centre before and he had strong social difficulties. We also told them we'd registered JB in a special school program.

Beyond the ADHD Label
One Mother's Struggle for Change

Initially, we had lengthy discussions with the school about the facilities they could offer him. After our first appointment, they didn't tell us whether they could meet his needs because they wanted to do more research. We were impressed.

They told us they would visit JB at day care and the special school to observe him in the schooling environment and have a face-to-face discussion with his current teachers.

After doing this, they called us back for a third appointment to advise that they would take him on if we continued to work with our psychologist and maintain open communication. Of course we agreed. They'd already shown us they were prepared to put in the hours to cater for him.

At the same time, we were interviewed by another school we'd sourced. The interview was a five minute one-on-one where we advised them that JB had some difficulties. They immediately told us that was fine and they could deal with that. A few weeks later, we received a letter advising that he was accepted.

When it came to choosing between the two schools, it was a no-brainer. We chose the school that put the time in to ensure

School issues

they knew what they were getting into. It turned out to be a great choice.

JB is now in Year 2 and these first two years have been quite challenging. We have had reduced hours where he's attended school for only half days or short weeks. He has spent time in other teachers' rooms and at the office where he has completed his work. He has been sent home when things have become too much for him. And sometimes he hasn't gone to school at all because his teacher hasn't been there.

So, as great as our school is, it hasn't been without teething problems, and I think you'll get that at most schools. We weren't happy when they sent JB home when things got too much; nor were we happy whenever he was sent to the office for disrupting the class, as he often ended up just playing with the iPad after finishing his work. He saw it as a reward.

We did trial an alternative school for what was supposed to be a week, but that was a failure. They had him for five hours before deciding he was too headstrong and they wouldn't be able to work with him. Although I understood their decision, it still hurt immensely. I felt very defeated at the time.

So JB went back to his usual school, and we sat down with them again and voiced our concerns. Strategies changed again and we implemented yet another form of discipline that he would work with. By the end of the year, we felt like we were on top of things again. Though I'm sure another year of school will bring all new challenges!

Communication with schools

It's imperative that you have a good relationship with your school. The lines of communication must be open on both sides to create the best school experience for your child.

Having regular meetings with people such as the teacher, learning support team and principal shows the school that you're an active parent willing to work with them to give your child the best education.

All this working with the school and going to meetings is definitely time consuming, but try to find the best thing that works for you. If you're working full time, it can be very hard to get to all the appointments, sort out school plans, etc.

School issues

Here are some ways you could work with the school while achieving a balance between supporting the school and working:

- Request early morning appointments before you go to work. This may see you only 30 minutes late for work, which may work better than leaving work in the middle of the day. Many schools won't do after-hours meetings, but you may find that early morning works for everyone.
- Have a phone conference with everyone if you can't get away from work. This may work better, as the appointment may be faster and you won't have travel time.
- Stay in touch with your teacher via email. Many teachers are now happy to provide email addresses so you'll always know what's happening. It may not be ideal for an IEP meeting, but may work for other communications.
- Where possible, schedule your appointments for annual leave time or rostered days off when you won't be pressured for time.

Tips for the working mum

Having a school-aged child with ADHD has its challenges, so you'll probably be called into school for various reasons. Whether your child is challenged socially or academically, you'll need to support them at school.

This will put enormous pressure on your working life. Here are some tips that could make life a little easier:

- Be honest with your employer. Tell them about your child's challenges, what you may need to do and the calls you may get from the school.
- If you do get a call up to the school, offer to complete your work from home where possible. Make sure you do get that work done, as it will put your employer's mind at ease and they'll trust you if you need to do it again.
- If you can't work from home, make up the time where possible. Be a fantastic employee so your employer is happy to give you the flexibility you need.
- If you can afford to, consider dropping your hours so you can be around at school more.

School issues

- If you have a business idea, consider building it and leaving employment. Having my own business has given me the flexibility to be there for my child that I didn't have in my job. This has been really hard work but rewarding for me personally as well.
- If you have a partner, share the workload. Take turns taking time off work to attend school appointments and other appointments. This will reduce both your stress and the amount of time you need to be away from work.

Other school options

If mainstream school doesn't work for your child—and, to be honest, it doesn't for most children living with ADHD—you may have other options depending on your circumstances and your area.

Home schooling

A lot of parents choose home schooling for their children these days. This option gives you the flexibility to teach your child by structuring the curriculum to suit their needs. There are many home-schooling options available, such as distance education, home schooling and unschooling. You'll need to research which one is best for your child.

If you work full time, you may not be able to consider this. However, if you have the ability, it is something you may wish to consider.

We've discussed it a few times in our house, but we haven't done it yet. It is something I keep in mind to consider if we get to that point. It does require a lot of time, but parents who do it tell me it's really rewarding for their children.

There may be many parents in your area who home school. If you're considering this option, it would be worth meeting up and discussing how it works for them. There are several Facebook groups where you can get support from other parents, so you're not alone.

Steiner school

A Steiner school teaches children through active learning, imitation and their own creative experience. Their learning is filled with stories, songs, creative play, interaction with nature and involvement in everyday human activities.

School issues

When you walk into a Steiner school, you get a sense of calm combined with a loving environment, as they teach children through gentle guidance and expression.

We attended a Steiner school open day and found it a beautiful, nurturing environment. It impressed me more than I'd expected it to.

However, I felt that my son (and I!) would be way too 'outgoing' for this type of environment. I remember saying to my mum, 'Gee, JB and I would be like the Tasmanian Devil in the cartoons running through a library!' This environment would never work for us, but I was impressed all the same.

Check the Steiner Education website to see if there's a school near you: http://www.steinereducation.edu.au/

Montessori

Montessori is not a school system but an approach to education. This is the way they describe this approach:

> *The Montessori approach to learning offers a broad vision of education as an 'aid to life', and aims to inspire children towards a lifelong love of learning, by following their natural developmental*

trajectory. Montessori classrooms provide a specially crafted learning environment where children are able to respond to their natural tendency to work. Within a framework of order, the children progress at their own pace and rhythm, according to their individual capabilities.

You'll find a wealth of information about the Montessori system on their website: http://montessori.org.au/

Personally, I was super impressed with the Montessori system and thought it was something that would work really well for JB. I arranged a class observation for an hour and was blown away by the calmness of the classroom and how the children worked together. And, although they were allowed to work on whatever they chose, the structure was still there. It was amazing.

I think their teaching style—keeping the same teacher for three years and allowing the children to set their own learning pace with guidance from teachers and peers—is a beautiful way to learn.

School issues

After some convincing, my husband agreed to have a look. He too was very impressed. And anyone who knows my husband knows he can be very cynical and doesn't like change much, so it was a lot for him to go there, let alone agree with their teaching style.

Although we loved the concept, we were unsure whether JB would be suited to this system. We decided to meet with the principal and be upfront about his needs to see what she thought. She too was apprehensive about the system working for JB but agreed to meet him.

After she met JB and we showed him around the school, we all agreed to do a five-day trial. I arranged for him to have a week off school and told them what we were doing, and then spent the next week talking JB through how the trial would work.

On the morning of the first day, JB and I chatted about what to expect. We drove the 30 minutes to the school and I answered lots of his questions on the way. All seemed well.

Then we arrived and, suddenly, JB didn't want to do it. It took all my effort just to get him to the classroom. It was a while before he let me leave, but eventually I was able to head home.

Beyond the ADHD Label
One Mother's Struggle for Change

At 12.30pm, the school called asking me to pick him up. I imagined that things weren't going well, but that I would pick him up early and return him again the next day. I was wrong.

The principal met me in the office and asked me to sit down. (Here we go!) She said, 'I'm sorry, your child isn't suited to our system.' My goodness, I was floored! He hadn't even lasted a day!

I was shattered—another option tried and failed. I was fast running out of options! I was extremely disappointed that they hadn't given the trial longer, but they knew their system better than I did and probably knew which children would and wouldn't fit.

But that was my experience; it doesn't mean *your* child wouldn't fit. If this sort of system appeals to you, it's definitely worth contacting them for a meeting.

Reconsidering your job

Realistically, helping your child get through school is going to take some of your time—perhaps a lot. So you may need to reconsider your work options.

School issues

Working for yourself isn't for everyone. For me, there were so many advantages to working for myself and I was in a position to do it. I feel very lucky that it's worked out well so far.

But if you can't start a business (or don't want to), try to find an employer that gets you and your family's needs. I was fortunate to have that but I still felt that I would continually let them down. I'm sure they would have had enough of my absences after a while.

But if you can create an understanding relationship with your employer, this will reduce so much pressure on you.

Beyond the ADHD Label
One Mother's Struggle for Change

Specialists

Specialists are experts in their particular field. Throughout your journey with ADHD, you'll learn to love them and sometimes hate them, but that's alright. Ultimately, they're there to help you though this and offer guidance and expertise.

It's vital to be happy with your specialist and feel they're on your side. If you don't feel a specialist is hearing you or working with you appropriately, you must speak up or find someone who does.

You'll probably have several different specialists throughout your child's ADHD journey. We have a team of specialists that we use. We've changed several of them over time, as I didn't feel some were working for us anymore.

Below is the list of specialists that we've worked with so far, but every path with ADHD is different. You may feel you need different types of specialists or not as many of them. Do what's right for you and your family and what works best.

Family doctor (GP)

Your family doctor or GP is one of the most important people to have a relationship with. This doctor will receive all the specialists' reports, keep your referrals up to date and, of course, be the person you turn to when you want to try new methods. I did a lot of research to choose the right doctor and, luckily, she was at the practice we already attended.

Our GP was a strong advocate for pushing to get the help we needed. She found the right specialists for us and we were happy with all of them (almost!). If I found something I wanted to try, I'd discuss it with her and we'd get it done.

For example, I had read about how lack of sleep or interrupted sleep patterns could present as ADHD symptoms, so I asked her to organise a sleep test, which she did. The test showed nothing, but it was another option we could eliminate as a possibility.

I also told her I wanted a hearing test done, and again she told me where to go and it was organised. I returned needing a referral to an ear, nose and throat doctor, which resulted in an operation to have adenoids out and grommets in. This made a bit of difference for JB.

Specialists

As your GP receives all the specialists' reports, you must also be able to discuss these outcomes with your GP and feel supported.

We recently changed GPs for JB, as I felt we'd exhausted our run with our existing one and I wanted one with a specific interest in ADHD. (Trust me, they do exist—you just have to find them.) When I finally found this doctor, his practice told me he wasn't taking any new clients. I said I was happy to wait and they could contact me when he was available—and they did!

I was confident that he knew about ADHD within five minutes of walking into his office. I was impressed and felt instantly comfortable. I'm still happy with him today.

It may take some time to find the right GP, but it's worth putting in the time. You need to know they're in your corner, that they have your child's best interest at heart, and don't just want you in and out of their office to get paid.

Consider all GPs—not just that ones who bulk bill. Yes, there is an added cost, but it's worth it to get the help you need. A lot of medical practices do bulk bill children anyway, but you shouldn't use this as the deciding factor when choosing your doctor—it's just a bonus. Choose one that will do what you ask them to do and will help you.

Here are some questions to ask a potential GP:

- What do you know about ADHD?
- What are your feelings about medication for ADHD?
- Are you happy to work with me and consider any suggestions I may have?
- Are you happy to work with other specialists and relay back to me what they've reported?

Ideally, you want to put a strong team together and your GP will be one of the key people in it.

Paediatrician

A paediatrician is a medical doctor who manages children's physical, behavioural and mental health from birth until the age of 16 or 18, depending on their practice. A paediatrician is

Specialists

trained to diagnose and treat a broad range of childhood illnesses from minor health problems to serious diseases.

It's essential to research the right paediatrician, as you definitely need to choose one who specialises in ADHD and child behaviours. There is absolutely no point in choosing a paediatrician who specialises in childhood asthma or childhood diseases. They will be no help to you.

To find my paediatrician, I just did an internet search for 'paediatrician and ADHD', which brought up private options in my area and I spoke to other parents for referrals as well.

Before you visit your GP for a referral, explore what's available and who you would like to see. Expect that they may not refer you to the one you've chosen, as that paediatrician may not be taking new patients. If you're informed about who the specialised paediatricians are, you and your GP can discuss who they will refer you to.

What to expect when booking a paediatrician

- If they're not taking new clients, you won't get in.

- If they are taking new clients, the wait time may be months or even years. (One paediatrician had an 18 month wait!)
- They may open their books for only one week twice a year, so you need to time it perfectly or put it in your diary to actually get an appointment.
- These statistics are based on the private health system; the public health system wait will be much longer.
- Expect to pay about $200–400 for a private paediatrician. If you're in Australia, Medicare will give you about $120 back, depending what you're paying.

Preparing for the appointment

If you've waited some time to see this paediatrician, you don't want to waste the appointment time.

So make sure you come armed with:

- letters or reports from the school explaining any problems the child is having or things they're concerned about
- a list of things that you've already put in place, like diet or behavioural strategies

Specialists

- a list of other specialists you may have consulted already—medical or natural
- any family history.

Your GP may also give you forms to complete.

Psychologist

Most children with some form of behavioural problem will be referred to a psychologist.

A psychologist evaluates and studies behaviour and mental processes. They work with your child usually in a one hour session every month or two, depending on your psychologist or your budget. They usually cost $0–85 per visit (after Medicare rebate if you're in Australia).

You will need a GP referral to see a psychologist if you want to claim the Medicare rebate. If you have private health insurance, you may be able to claim part of the visit without a doctor's referral.

Note that a psychologist can't write scripts for medication; you'll need to get those from a paediatrician, psychiatrist or GP.

A psychologist may work with you and your child by:

- providing teaching strategies for handling different social situations at school
- talking through problems that your child may be experiencing
- helping you with parenting strategies and handling specific situations
- working with schools on what's happening in the classroom.

If you can arrange for your psychologist to visit your child's school and observe them in the classroom, this will help immensely. However, you'll need to pay full fees for this, as Medicare won't cover this service.

Having the psychologist assess the happenings at school gives them a better understanding of what's occurring. Additionally, they can talk with the teacher to understand further.

You may also have a psychologist who is licensed in the Positive Parenting Program (Triple P). You can read more about this program in the chapter on 'Strategies and programs'.

Specialists

The psychologist is one of the most important people to have on your team. They're likely to give you the most beneficial strategies and work with you on a more tailored-needs basis.

Psychiatrist

A psychiatrist is a physician who specialises in diagnosing and treating mental disorders.

Psychiatrists are medical doctors—so different from psychologists—who must evaluate patients to determine whether their symptoms are the result of a physical illness, psychiatric illness or combination of both. A psychiatrist can prescribe medication.

You may choose to have a psychiatrist rather than a paediatrician, and that's fine. We do this ourselves. A specialised (private) psychiatrist generally has less wait time than a paediatrician.

A psychiatrist will work with your child and discuss their concerns. A good one will also work with your school, and be a constant contact for anything you and your school are concerned about.

We use our psychiatrist as the 'head of our team' and everything runs through her. We keep her up to date on any new strategies in place. She is across all our specialists and remains in constant contact with the school so she knows what's going on.

As with all your specialists, ensure you have a good relationship with the psychiatrist so you and your school can contact them at any time with concerns. Also ensure the psychiatrist is happy to work with the rest of the team.

Discuss the idea of medication in detail, if that's the route you need to go down. Make sure you understand everything: what to expect, side effects, how to contact the psychiatrist if you have any questions, what the school needs to look for, everything! If you don't have this relationship, you need to find someone you can work with like this.

Dietician/nutritionist

Differences between them

Before we continue, let's clarify the difference between a dietician and nutritionist. Following is the difference according to Deakin University[6]:

Dieticians:

Specialists

Dietitians are health professionals specialising in food and nutrition who have received clinical training to prescribe special diets for medical conditions. Dietitians hold qualifications that allow them to work in the hospital, community or private practice setting. These qualifications generally consist of a three-year science degree followed by an 18 month - 2-year Master's degree in nutrition and dietetics or a 4-year undergraduate program with a significant workplace placement in the final year.

All dietitians can call themselves nutritionists if they choose as they have university qualifications in nutrition; however, not all nutritionists could be considered to be dietitians. A dietitian in addition to, or as part of their qualification in human nutrition has undertaken a course of study that included substantial theory and supervised and assessed professional dietetic practice in clinical practice (hospital based), food service management and community nutrition.

Dietitians are eligible for membership of the Dietitians Association of Australia (DAA) and to participate in the Accredited Practising Dietitians (APD) and/or Accredited Nutritionist *(AN) program. The titles APD and AN are protected by law. Only qualified practitioners who have met certain requirements can use this title.*

Nutritionists:

Nutritionists design, coordinate, implement and evaluate a range of population health interventions to improve the wellbeing of individuals, communities and the population as a whole through better food and nutrition. There are a diverse range of qualifications that can lead to people calling themselves a nutritionist. A nutritionist may have a

Specialists

> *Bachelor-level degree with majors in nutrition or a postgraduate degree such as Graduate Certificate, Graduate Diploma, Master's Degree or even a PhD specialising in nutrition.*
>
> *Some people call themselves nutritionists even though they do not have suitable qualifications as there is no legal protection of the title 'nutritionist'. Voluntary registration systems do exist through the Nutrition Society of Australia (NSA) and this will help support the profession and its development into the future.*

How they can help

Whether you decide to go with a dietician or nutritionist, either is likely to assist you. We chose a dietician, but first we eliminated all numbers and preservatives.

While, obviously, no one diet has the ability to 'cure' ADHD (wouldn't that be a simple fix?), it may certainly help alleviate some symptoms.

We chose our dietician purely because we wanted to do the failsafe diet, designed by Sue Dengate. (You can read about our journey with the failsafe diet in the chapter on 'The food question'.) My dietician was familiar with the failsafe diet and could make sure I was doing it properly, as I wanted to take this seriously.

You need to do your own research and decide the best option for you.

Occupational therapist

An occupational therapist (OT) enables people to participate in the activities of everyday life. They can work in schools, aged care homes, acute care units, mental health units and injury management centres.

OTs can help children work to achieve developmental milestones, such as fine motor skills and hand–eye coordination. They can educate parents on helping children with normal development and learning.

For a child living with ADHD, an OT can help with:

- fine motor skills
- handwriting

Specialists

- social skills
- play skills
- sensory processing issues
- gross motor skills
- perception
- strategies for adapting to different scenarios.

We've had a lot of success with our more recent occupational therapist. It's not unusual to walk into her office and find her looking dishevelled and miserable just to create a different expected environment for JB and see how he handles it.

She then role-plays with him, trying to get him to respond to this different environment. It's amazing to see how he reacts, and then we talk about how he reacted and what to expect after the role play has finished.

She teaches him to identify with his feelings. We use a reference, such as characters from *Winnie-the-Pooh*: Piglet if he's anxious or scared; Rabbit if he's angry; Tigger if his mood is up and he's bouncing about the place; Winnie-the-Pooh if he's feeling 'just right'; and Eeyore if he's down or sad. (Though Tigger seems to live at our house *a lot*! As he probably does at yours too.)

Beyond the ADHD Label
One Mother's Struggle for Change

Even these little strategies help us immensely. JB has learned to identify his own feelings and sometimes tells me when he's feeling like one of them. I also use these references and remind him where is supposed to be feeling.

Another great strategy the OT teaches is rocking. I'm sure you can relate to how your child's behaviour can escalate when you're out to dinner where the situation and environment are unusual. (Once, JB was literally standing on his head and being a caterpillar on the booth seats, as he just couldn't sit still!)

I had always struggled to deal with this until our OT taught us about rocking. If we're out and things are escalating, I ask JB to identify his behaviour and if he needs to be rocked. He usually says yes, so I lie him down across my knees and either rock him from side to side or dip him up and down, depending on what he feels he needs. I combine this with either 'brushing' him with my hands on his skin or gently stroking him with my fingernails (a good excuse to get your nails professionally done), which he loves.

It may take some time for him to come down and be calm, but generally it works. It's a godsend when we're out. Yes, I do get

Specialists

some funny looks, but they're much better than the judgmental looks from people who think you're a bad parent!

I strongly recommend at least trying an OT to see if they'll work for you. It's one of the best things we've done.

Make sure you get one that works for you and understands your child. We did try an OT unsuccessfully in the early days—either it wasn't right for us at the time or she wasn't the right person...who knows? But we have one now and it's fantastic.

OTs are under the Medicare limit and may cost you about $75 a visit, depending on the OT. The session usually lasts one hour and you get about $30 back from Medicare. However, they allow only five visits per year under this scheme. If you want more after that, you'll need to pay full price.

However, an exception to this rule is that you can have a mental health-trained OT and they can be referred under the mental health care plan for 10 sessions just like a psychologist.

Naturopath

A naturopath takes a holistic approach to health and provides an alternative medicine using natural remedies.

Beyond the ADHD Label
One Mother's Struggle for Change

You may not have visited a naturopath before because you're not sure what to expect. Personally, I think they're worthwhile to visit and consider—if not for a total treatment, then as an addition to the treatment you're doing.

Naturopaths can provide homeopathy, herbalism, acupuncture, iridology, diet and nutritional advice, life coaching and hypnotherapy.

Our naturopath experience

I took JB to see a well-known naturopath who specialises in iridology, dietetics, nutrition, homoeopathy, counselling, herbal medicine and homeopathy just to name a few. I researched him extensively when he was recommended and spoke with him several times before making the trip to see him.

Within about 10 minutes, he had pinpointed JB exactly. I was impressed. After chatting for another 40 minutes, he sent us home with tablets and herbs to try. Of course I didn't expect miracles, as it was going to take time.

I had warned the naturopath that there was no way JB would take anything that tasted disgusting, so we used items that weren't terribly bad— a high-quality, chewable multi-vitamin

Specialists

and homeopathic tablets rather than terrible-tasting herbs—and found creative ways to give them to him. This battle was nothing compared to the medication battle!

We saw a little change in behaviour as a result of this but not a massive amount. Still, I was much more comfortable trying this than the medication and clearly JB was too.

The naturopath also moved us onto a gluten- and dairy-free diet, which we tried for a few weeks. However, as you read earlier in the book, this excluded JB from his peers even more and wasn't worth the daily battle to get him to eat different foods.

Choosing a naturopath

If you've never used a naturopath before, look carefully. Ask people to recommend someone. You probably know someone who knows a good naturopath.

Then research them as much as you can. Make sure they have good reviews and have done the appropriate studies. If you can find one who specialises in behavioural therapies, this is a huge bonus.

Here are some tips for finding a good, even great, naturopath:

- Research, research, research!
- Ask friends and family for recommendations.
- Make sure they've done the appropriate qualifications—which should be on their website.
- See if they're a member of an association, such as the Australian Natural Therapists Association. This means they're monitored and their training has to reach a certain standard before they're allowed to be a member.
- If you're a member of a health fund, this could be a helpful deciding factor as well.
- Call and talk to your chosen naturopath. Discuss what you want help with and what you're looking for, and find out if they can help you.
- Trust your instincts. If you think this is the right person to go with, make an appointment.

At the appointment

Firstly, the naturopath will probably ask about your family history and go through it extensively. Make sure you're armed with these details and all the information from the specialists you've seen.

Specialists

Don't expect a visit to the naturopath to be like seeing the doctor. They will ask you questions that your doctor hasn't asked you before. They may also want to do tests that you think are out of the ordinary. Naturopaths think differently than doctors, so they need different types of information.

They're likely to give you things that don't taste great. If your child is young, talk to the naturopath about alternatives to the remedies they're giving you. You don't want to pay for a huge number of remedies that your child will refuse to take.

Your health fund will pay only a portion of the consultation and none towards the remedies, so this will be an out-of-pocket expense.

Finally, don't expect the naturopath to have an all-in solution; however, they may help reduce a few problem behaviours. You can only give them a try.

Beyond the ADHD Label
One Mother's Struggle for Change

Programs and strategies

We've tried various programs and strategies to help JB and we've had varying results. In this section, I'll outline our experience with some of them so you know what's out there and can decide what to investigate for yourself.

Positive Parenting Program (Triple P)

Triple P[7] is a parenting program that gives parents tips for managing the everyday problems of family life—whether your children are toddlers or teenagers. This could include issues around self-esteem, tantrums and technology. You can read more about it on their website, www.triplep.net.

I'll be honest here. Although this is a pretty good program, you really need to tailor it to *your* child. I did the program three times and it was only the last time that I got something out of it. This is because our school's guidance counsellor is a program facilitator, so she tailored it to suit JB after I said it wasn't working for us.

My tip is to find a program that can be tailored for your child. Triple P does offer courses tailored to these children, which I hadn't found while I was doing it, but a more detailed search may find you a suitable course facilitator.

Behavioural therapy

Behavioural therapy can help a child living with ADHD understand their behaviour, and how it affects others and makes them feel. A specialist usually works with the child to help them identify their feelings and the consequences that their behaviour can have.

> *You may not get a behavioural therapist specifically. Your psychologist or occupational therapist might help your child with behaviour therapy or you may use a therapist that specialises in behaviour therapy. We found that our psychologist does this.*

The specialist who does the behavioural therapy will work with you and your child to develop a plan tailored to their needs. They'll discuss coping mechanisms with your child, role-play different situations they may encounter, teach relaxation methods and social skills, and more.

Programs and strategies

They'll probably work with you as well to give you strategies for guiding your child through various situations.

Sleep therapy

If you have a child living with ADHD, you know all about sleep problems—jumping on the bed at 9.30pm and not going to sleep. Making every excuse under the sun not to go to bed. Your child might even experience sleep disruptions, which also disrupts the next day because they're still tired.

Sometimes disruptive sleep patterns are mistaken for ADHD behaviour, so it's worth looking into if you have these issues.

Getting a sleep test

After reading about the sleep patterns of ADHD children, I asked the doctor to refer JB to the sleep clinic. After visiting a specialised paediatrician, I booked JB into the hospital for the sleep test. We were asked lots of questions like 'Does he snore?', 'Does he sleep with his mouth open?', 'What are his sleep patterns like in general?', 'Does he suffer nightmares and night terrors?' and other questions relating to sleep patterns.

We arrived at the hospital in the late afternoon and they quickly showed us to the room where we would spend the night. JB was only six at the time, so making this a fun experience was imperative. We took some games with us and made sure we could watch TV there. It was exciting for him to choose what food he would eat in the morning and he asked the poor nurses a million questions as he was wired up to the machine. He actually dealt with it extremely well and understood what was happening the whole time.

In the end, everything showed up as normal, but it was worth checking.

Helping your child get restful sleep

Lack of sleep can escalate ADHD symptoms, so getting the right amount of sleep is important.

- Set a bedtime routine and keep to it as much as possible. Life doesn't always go to plan when you have a child living with ADHD, but sticking to a bedtime routine will help. They'll know what to expect every night and respond better to going to bed.
- Take time to read to them or just lie with them and have a chat before they go to sleep. This will help them wind down.

Programs and strategies

- Ensure the bedroom is set up for sleep. Use heavy curtains or blinds to block out the light. Ensure there are no brightly lit digital clocks or clock lights—or turn them away from the bed—as well as televisions and computers.
- If your child needs a night light, make sure it's a true night light that uses soft lighting to get them through the night.
- Try relaxation techniques, such as rocking or brushing:
    - One brushing technique involves using a soft bristle brush to brush up and down your child's arms and legs. This helps with circulation and settling.
    - Rocking can be done on a yoga ball or just over your lap. Simply put your child on their stomach and rock them by dipping them up and down. This 'rebalances' their system and settles them down.

We use several of these techniques; and, if JB is on a high before bed, we use them all.

If you suspect that your child may have sleep disruptions, it's very important to speak to your doctor and get it checked out.

SleepTalk®

SleepTalk® is a process where you talk to your child while they sleep[8]. It's designed to get into their subconscious and boost their confidence.

The concept involves rousing your child to a certain sleep awareness—not to wake them but to reactivate their subconscious. Then you talk to your child in a positive manner, so the message gets into the subconscious and they start thinking accordingly when they're awake.

The SleepTalk® people have consultants who can help you through this and a book with step-by-step instructions.

This is a relatively new process for us, and something we're still trialling and understanding. As a mother, I prefer to teach my son to see the positives in life rather than dwell on the negatives, so this is definitely something that appeals to me.

Allergy testing

Allergy testing involves conducting tests to see if the body reacts to food, chemicals, grasses or other environmental factors. Some allergic reactions can cause some ADHD symptoms.

Programs and strategies

Allergy testing works very well together with the diet changes mentioned earlier in this book. Allergy tests examine the body for issues that can't be found through normal testing, particularly food allergies. The most common allergies are milk, egg, peanut, wheat, soybean, fish and shellfish.

As I mentioned in the section on diet, you can see changes in a child's behaviour when they eat certain foods (and sugar is a common one with kids). These can trigger new symptoms that present as ADHD or escalate ADHD symptoms that your child already has. So it's really important to examine this further to potentially reduce the severity of some behaviours.

Although your child's skin may not present as having an allergic reaction to a food or chemical, a reaction may occur within their body that you can't see.

If your child lives with ADHD and you see signs that may be an allergy, get your child evaluated. Properly managing allergic problems may help them respond better to ADHD treatment.

You'll need a doctor's referral to arrange allergy testing, as a specialist will need to do it.

If the specialist does find allergies and prescribes medication, be aware that some of the medication's side effects may adversely affect your child's ADHD symptoms or their ADHD medication. Discuss this with your doctor.

Animal-assisted therapy

Animal-assisted therapy can help with social, emotional and cognitive functioning.

Some of us already know how nice it is to have an animal in the house. Now think about how it would be for someone whose world feels like a crazy mess. Probably calming, right?

It can be amazing to have an animal help your child through life. And animal therapy doesn't have to involve a dog; you can do equine therapy (horses) or even dolphin therapy.

Currently, not many people in Australia use dogs for ADHD. However, many people around the world are using dogs to help children with autism and animal treatment for ADHD is becoming more prevalent.

We recently introduced a therapy dog to our house and, within a week, we could see a huge difference in JB's anxiety. You can read more about our therapy dog in the next chapter and follow my Facebook page for updates on how it's all going.

Programs and strategies

How therapy animals are used

Therapy dogs are commonly used for veterans suffering post-traumatic stress disorder (PTSD), so there's no reason it wouldn't help children living with ADHD. Dogs used to help PTSD sufferers are trained to detect their owner's emotions and signs of anxiety. On sensing this anxiety, they react to get their owner's attention to comfort them and divert their attention from whatever they're focused on.

In equine therapy, the horse has the ability to mirror the owner's emotions. As the owner interacts with the horse, they learn to observe and respond to the horse's behaviour instead of being stuck in their pattern of behaviour. Children find this type of therapy fun and something different to do.

There are many ways to use animal-assisted therapy, so find out what's best for you. There may be a psychologist or psychiatrist near you who works with dogs or horses and provides this type of service. Or you may choose to get a dog to train as a therapy dog.

I've heard that cats have worked for some people as well. A cat has a calming effect on a child. Some schools use guinea pigs to help with anxiety and use time with the animal as a reward for the children.

So if your child isn't a dog person, another option may work for you.

Training the animal

Don't be scared off by the cost of a therapy animal. Admittedly, training a true certified therapy dog costs around $30,000. However, if you do your research and you don't need the certification, you can use personal trainers to help you with the skills your dog requires.

Certification does allow you to take the dog into public places, but this might not be an issue for you or you may be able to work around it. You might just want an animal at home to help settle your child.

It's very important to start basic obedience training as soon as possible to cover the basics before you get to the therapy training.

A few associations in Australia provide the skills to train a therapy dog and some run affordable courses. You can also google 'therapy dog trainers' to find one who is skilled in this area and has an affordable hourly rate.

Programs and strategies

Beware: Many trainers claim to be therapy dog trainers but aren't and they really have no idea how to do it. It's important to choose wisely, as you don't want the dog learning bad habits early.

Bringing a therapy puppy home

Here are some tips for bringing home a puppy for your child living with ADHD:

1. Have your child bond with the puppy as much as possible before it comes home. Ask the breeder if you can do several visits to start building that bond. If they say no, I would seriously consider whether they're the right breeder to purchase from.

2. Explain the rules to your child. Make sure they understand their responsibilities before the dog comes home. If it helps, create a chart to remind them what they have to do.

3. Get an enclosure or cage where the dog can go rest. Explain to the child that this is where the puppy will have its rest time and that they must leave the puppy alone when it's in there. This is important, as puppies need lots of sleep.

4. Involve your child as much as possible. Take them to vet visits and dog obedience classes if possible (as most will allow this but may not let them handle the dog). Teach them to feed the dog, pick up the poop, walk them (once the puppy masters the leash), brush them and play with them safely.
5. Have fun but be careful. We know that puppies can get carried away and bite. Teach your child to stop the dog getting carried away by saying 'Stop' or 'No', and just walking away and ignoring the dog. Sourcing a good therapy dog trainer will help you with all of this, as your child will need training as well.

Outside school activities

If you have a child living with ADHD, you may have found that getting them into a group or team activity, such as soccer, football, dancing or music, just isn't working. Have you found that coaches just don't understand your child? Maybe you've already been asked to leave that environment. You might be thinking that the only fun activity you can offer your child is something they can do on their own.

Programs and strategies

We had exactly this experience. When JB was three, it was suggested that we not renew our paid lessons for soccer. We were also asked to leave two dance crews and I removed him from a drama school myself because I knew it was only a matter of time.

Telling a child that they're not allowed to return to the class they love is heartbreaking. How do you tell them they can't come back because they're 'too naughty'? I was terrified that JB would develop a complex that people didn't want him.

When we were 'asked to leave' our fourth place, I had had enough! I simply told him he wasn't behaving in these classes and that's why he couldn't go back. He was heartbroken, as he'd particularly enjoyed that last class and made a nice friend.

When I enrolled JB in groups, I was always honest, telling them he could be a bit of a handful. They always assured me they would manage, including this last time. A young girl was taking the class and I could tell from the first lesson that she would struggle to control him.

After a few lessons, on the afternoon we were due for another class, the centre called asking us not to come back. I was mortified, as they hadn't once spoken to me about any

Beyond the ADHD Label
One Mother's Struggle for Change

problems, even though I had warned them. I was not impressed.

After the phone call, I had my cry and collected JB from school. I told him he wasn't going that afternoon and he cried all the way home. He just didn't understand why he couldn't go. I had told him that he needed to behave, but he just said 'I can't help it, I get so excited because I love it'. What could I say? It was horrible.

After that, I left it a while before thinking about outside school activities again. I was over JB being rejected and figured JB was too. However, he kept asking me when he was going to play football, join a dance crew and learn music, so I had to find a solution.

I decided to find a teacher who was good at working with children with ADHD and provided one-on-one lessons. One of my employees mentioned that her mum was a music teacher and used to dealing with children like JB. I gave her a call immediately and had a good chat about my situation. By the end, I was comfortable that she could teach him music.

Dance was my next challenge. Traditionally, dance classes are held in groups, so I thought finding a one-on-one dance

Programs and strategies

teacher at an affordable price might be a tad difficult. But not so. I emailed three dance schools about my dilemma and they all replied that they could help.

We chose a local hip hop and breakdance class and arranged for the teacher to teach a one-on-one class before the group class. I was a little worried at first because the teacher was still in school himself and we didn't have a great track record with young teachers. However, he was very patient with JB and a great teacher, so we are still with him today. *And* it only costs me $20 per lesson. Perfect.

We had the same experience with football. I chatted to the coach and he agreed to hold a few lessons for JB free of charge to see how he went. In the end, JB didn't actually like football so he decided not to return himself.

You may be having similar problems getting suitable lessons for your child in activities they want to do. My advice is to get on the phone and call people. Don't be afraid to ask or to admit that your child lives with ADHD. If they don't know, they won't handle them correctly and it won't be enjoyable for your child at all.

Beyond the ADHD Label
One Mother's Struggle for Change

Hopefully, they'll be honest with you if you're honest with them. They'll tell you if they don't think they can teach your child and won't take them on. Trust me, only a few will be this honest, as most will say they can handle them but don't understand ADHD enough to know what they're agreeing to.

I also recommend helping out wherever you can. If you do, they'll consider you a valuable parent and do what it takes to make things work, and not just dump your child when it gets too hard. You can also give them strategies that may work if you see they're not coping.

Don't be afraid to bring problems to the teacher's attention—you're paying for their time and bringing them business.

Our children have as much right to do outside school activities as other children; they just need a little more attention to get them through. Finding the right school, team or club is the answer. When you do, you won't look back. Your child will benefit from activities with new children outside school and thrive on learning another skill that keeps them occupied.

Programs and strategies

Note: When you have a child living with ADHD, you can feel when something is working really well. But then, suddenly, things will change and what was working will stop working. You always need to be thinking of new strategies to implement. Nothing will ever stay the same.

The strategies and programs I've outlined in this chapter are a starting point for you and your child. I've let you know our experiences with them but you may have different experiences.

By all means, give these strategies and programs a try, but make sure they suit your child's particular needs rather than being a one-size-fits-all. And speak to the experts before you make any decision.

Beyond the ADHD Label
One Mother's Struggle for Change

Doggie therapy

In the previous chapter, you read about the value of animal-assisted therapy in helping a child living with ADHD. We've just started our journey with our therapy dog, River, and it's been a fun and interesting experience so far.

In this chapter, I'll provide more detail about how we chose this dog and how the therapy is progressing to give you an idea of what's involved.

Deciding to get a therapy dog

We had wondered for a while whether a dog could help JB live with his ADHD. We had done a group therapy session with a local psychologist who used therapy dogs in her sessions. Over the five weeks, the change we saw in JB was amazing. So we started looking into it.

I researched how having a therapy dog could help JB, how we would train one, the right breed to choose and how JB would handle having a dog.

We did already have a dog but, unfortunately, that particular breed and JB's energy did not mix. The dog literally decided to pack up and leave our household, moving in with my parents who lived on our block!

So we knew that choosing the right breed was essential.

Choosing the breed

We didn't have the backyard for a big breed (as we have lots of beautiful gardens), so it had to be a small to medium dog. However, many small breeds can get snippy with big, boisterous children. We love our collie breeds so we looked at Shetland Sheepdogs (Miniature Collies) and Border Collies. I also considered a Cavalier King Charles Spaniel, as they're quite smart and placid, but my husband doesn't like spaniels.

Ultimately, the dog had to be smart, robust and set up to be a therapy dog of sorts. I wasn't looking for a full-on therapy dog in the true sense, as I couldn't afford it. I wanted a dog that I could train myself (with help) to help my son through the tough times and be his friend when none were around.

Doggie therapy

If you decide to get a dog for your child living with ADHD, find a dog that is hardy, can put up with their energy, and won't shy away or be scared of your child and vice versa—otherwise it defeats the purpose of having the dog.

After a few months of speaking with breeders, we decided on a Border Collie. I even found a breeder whose dogs had therapy dogs in their bloodline. So we visited those puppies and chose one, and the bonding began.

Introducing the puppy

You may think that Border Collies have too much energy and, for some families, you may be right. However, JB is on the go all the time and it's like a competition to see who can run out of energy first!

We decided on a male as they tend to be more affectionate. His name was River. We loved him instantly and knew he was the one for us.

To start the bonding process, we drove out to the breeder's house every fortnight once the puppy was four weeks old. This is an important process, and a good breeder should encourage these visits to ensure that you, your family and the dog are comfortable with each other before they come home.

JB was so excited to head out there to play with him and run about. You could really see the bond forming.

Once River was 11 weeks old, he was allowed to come home. JB was beside himself with excitement. He told everyone he was getting a new puppy—we could see the pride and sense of responsibility kicking in.

Training the puppy - and us!

Then River was home and this was where the training really started—for the puppy and for JB. My son had to learn to be gentle, and we all know that teaching a child living with ADHD to be gentle can be like leading an elephant through a glassware shop.

There was lots of 'reminding' that the puppy was only little, so he couldn't be treated roughly. And more reminding that the puppy couldn't run *all* the time and needed his sleep.

We also taught JB about feeding him, picking up poop in the garden (the job he was least impressed with) and taking trips to the vet to get the puppy checked. All the tasks that JB had to be involved with.

But then we had to start puppy school—for both of them. We're currently into more advanced puppy training and have had to remove JB from the training process. The bond between them is so incredibly strong that the dog won't do anything or listen to the handler if JB is at a training session. He just wants to be wherever JB is.

So I'll continue with River's obedience training and work with JB and River at home so they can learn it together. JB will join us when we move to the specialised therapy training. Luckily I found a trainer close to me and we'll be starting that soon.

The downside

Despite all the fun that our therapy dog has brought us, we've had some trying moments and, at times, I wonder if we've done the right thing. I've given myself so much more to do!

For starters, I have to find time to walk the dog every day. At the moment, I get up early in the morning and walk him for about one hour per day. That's a commitment that anyone makes when they choose a breed like a Border Collie. I'm fortunate to be working from home, so we have a routine, as

Beyond the ADHD Label
One Mother's Struggle for Change

I can definitely see the effect on the dog when his morning walk doesn't happen.

Additionally, we have to make sure the dog is fed properly (and I choose to make my own dog food). Having such a smart dog, I have to constantly create little puzzles for him to work out to get to his food. This keeps his brain ticking and stops him getting bored. All this takes even more time.

Finding the right obedience school is important as well. Our psychologist who does the dog therapy recommended we try a few different schools to see what works. They all have different styles and we needed to find one that worked for us and our child.

If you go this way, you may want your child to be involved in the training initially or you may like to do the training first and then teach your child how to handle the dog. This depends on the child's age and how they manage the dog.

Once puppy school was over and we got to the serious obedience training, bringing JB into the class just didn't work. He was just too young and needed lots of training in handling the dog correctly. Currently we feel that, if we can work with the dog ourselves first, we're halfway there for when we start

Doggie therapy

the therapy training. The therapy dog trainer will then help us train JB to handle the dog as well. After all, they have to work together.

Remember, depending what breed you choose, it can take 12 to 24 months for your dog to mature. So, for a while, you'll have a child with ADHD and a puppy!

Getting a therapy animal can be really tiring for a while and we're still going through this ourselves. One day I hope to be able to say it was all worth it, but at the moment I can't. (But I'm confident it will be!)

Beyond the ADHD Label
One Mother's Struggle for Change

Mindset

Mindset is all about the way you think. This can affect everything—the way you feel, your attitude to life, and how you interact with and react to others.

Sitting with a negative mindset is no good for anyone. You can start to feel bogged down with sad and depressive emotions, causing you to make inadequate decisions, ignore your health and feel unable to cope with situations.

We can all get into a negative way of thinking (with or without a child with ADHD!) but learning to pull yourself out of this mindset is empowering, as you can achieve anything once you do.

My own battle

As you know from my story earlier, I've battled with my own negative mindset. Things obviously aren't going well when you're crying in your car and locking yourself in toilets at shopping centres.

When JB was expelled from day care, I felt like my world had crashed—I saw only the negative in everything. I was scared that another day care wouldn't accept him; I worried how a school would react in the future when I told them he'd already been expelled; and I believed that people would judge me because of it. Day and night, I thought only of the bad things that would come of this. I felt sick with stress.

Eventually I hit the wall. I couldn't go on thinking this way because I wouldn't be able to help JB. And I would fall apart from the stress.

When I was a teenager, I suffered depression, which saw me in hospital at rock bottom. So when JB's problems started to overwhelm me, I knew what to look for and swore there was no way I would end up there again. I knew I needed to do everything possible to change my thinking.

It took time. I love self-help books and, being a financial planner, I enjoy reading books about money that also touch on self-help and positive mindset. During this time, I also read everything I could about ADHD and started educating myself so I felt ready to take on the world. I also downloaded podcasts by Oprah and others about self-help, self-belief and changing the way you look at life, and regularly listened to them in the car.

Mindset

I also started looking for a new day care centre for JB, deciding this might be a better move for him. If I took my time and chose the right centre, it would be a massive step forward for us. And it was!

After looking at several centres and discussing JB's needs in detail, we decided on one. The teacher was incredible. She saw JB for who he was and what he could do, and not the behaviour. First negative belief changed.

Then we had to find a school. I went in with the same plan—be honest and the right school will come. And it did. After going through the process, I was confident that we'd chosen the right school, as they were already aware of the problems they were working with. Next negative belief changed!

Worrying that people would judge me was a much harder negative belief to change. I still have to work on it occasionally, but definitely not as hard as I did. I believe that your mindset and beliefs need to be worked on every day to keep that positive flow. This work can involve a simple affirmation or listening to a podcast.

> *I've decided that what happens to my child is nobody's business and their opinions have nothing to do with me. Why should I worry what other people think when they don't know the story or the process that leads me to make decisions for him? This realisation has made a massive positive change to my life.*

Examining your own mindset

Attaining and keeping a positive mindset is one of the harder things about living with a child with ADHD, as you need to work on it every day. Booking appointments for your child and helping them through the therapies they need is easy compared with changing the way you think and your beliefs.

You may not think this requires much work but, trust me, it does. It takes a long time to get out of negative patterns of thinking and start seeing the positive. You may do it without realising you are!

Here are my tips for starting to change your mindset today.

Mindset

Catch your thoughts

The moment you catch yourself thinking negatively, stop and turn that thought around. You may have been sitting in that thought for hours without realising you were doing it! That's OK, just act on it as soon as it comes to your attention. Think about the other side of the situation. It can be absolutely anything as long as it's positive.

For example, JB was being particularly difficult and I realised I was spiralling into the 'Why me?' and 'Why do I have to deal with this?' thinking. Once I realised, I changed it to 'I'm dealing with this the best I can and I have all the knowledge I need right now to help him through the way he's thinking'.

This was something simple that helped me, but you may think of something else that helps you. It doesn't even have to be completely relevant at the time, as long as you get into the habit of changing that negative mindset as soon as you notice it.

Surround yourself with positive and supportive people

How can you be a positive person when you're surrounded by people who constantly whinge about their life and get stuck in their 'Why me?' story?

Beyond the ADHD Label
One Mother's Struggle for Change

If you find that you're 'stuck with' people who constantly talk about the negatives in their life—like family or close friends whom you don't want to move away from—you can work with that. When they start whinging, look for the positive side of the story and bring that to their attention. Still be a sympathetic ear and a good friend, but help them turn their way of thinking to the positive as well.

(Of course, we're not talking about the important life conversations that should be had for the sake of our sanity. Sometimes we just need to vent and get it all out. We're talking about the non-stop complaining that some people start as soon as they set eyes on you. You know the ones!)

If they don't like you doing this, they'll probably stop talking to you about negative things. That's great, as you don't need other people's negativity and drama when you're trying to maintain a positive outlook on life. It's a win–win—you keep your friend around but they don't use you as a sounding board to whinge at. And maybe, by example, you'll start turning around their way of thinking!

Mindset

Accept the hard days

There will be times when you don't want to deal with life that day. This is perfectly fine; we all get there at some point. When this happens, just do the best you can and reassess later.

Don't try to be perfect. Just accept that some days will be like this in your journey with ADHD.

Have a good cry

Sometimes we have to fall to pieces to be ready for the next step.

After a particularly hard morning dropping JB off to school, I found myself sobbing inconsolably all the way to my appointment. I just couldn't cope. But after I calmed down from the sobbing, I thought about how I could've dealt with the morning better and what I could take from it.

At this time, I had one of the biggest breakthroughs of my journey so far and started to feel more positive. Sometimes this needs to happen so we can open ourselves up to something new.

So it's OK to have a good cry and 'get it all out' if you use it to come out the other side. Once you've settled down, consider the situation that resulted in the final breakdown and how you handled it. Then think of another or a better way you might have handled it. You'll generally find the answers come to you easily.

Embracing the process

If you embrace the process of attaining and keeping a positive mindset, you'll find it does some incredible things for you. But don't expect it to happen overnight. This is an ongoing process that you'll need to work on for the rest of your life.

If you want to learn more on the subject, you can read self-help books, listen to self-help podcasts or watch videos on YouTube. Oprah has some great podcasts about personal growth.

Of course, sometimes you won't want to work on positive thinking at all. You'll just want to sit in your negative mindset for a while. And that's OK, as long as you don't sit there for too long. After a while, you'll risk losing that sense of positivity and self-worth you've already achieved.

Be kind to yourself and then, when you can, get out of your rut and keep moving forward. Go for a walk or play some music and dance around the house like nobody's watching (and who cares if they are!). Have a bath, have a massage or do anything

Mindset

that makes you feel a bit better than when you're sitting in the negative.

One step is all it takes and you can only do the best that you're able to do at the time.

Beyond the ADHD Label
One Mother's Struggle for Change

Where are we now?

As things stand

It seems like a lifetime ago that I sat in that director's office at JB's day care being asked to leave. How that meeting changed my life!

JB is now seven years old and we still have our bad days. Some days are really bad and I just want to crawl under a rock and never reappear. I've learned that I need to move on from these days and keep going.

I've chosen to look at ADHD as a positive thing in our lives and accept that there will be bad days. However, most of them are good and we're very equipped to deal with the bad days when they come.

At the time of writing, JB is under the guidance of a psychologist, psychiatrist and occupational therapist. We've also started training our dog to be a therapy dog. This dog is working wonders for our son.

Beyond the ADHD Label
One Mother's Struggle for Change

We now have enough experience to confidently sit with JB's new school teacher for the year and discuss what has worked, what hasn't worked and what we'd like to implement.

We've found private music and dance teachers, both of whom are working out really well. Now, when JB joins any new group, I speak extensively with the teacher to make sure they can handle him—not just *think* they can because they want the business. This really isn't their fault; they just don't understand ADHD.

Importantly, I rely heavily on my instincts today, not just in choosing groups and teachers, but in every situation. As parents, we need to be confident within ourselves and willing to speak openly about ADHD to get the knowledge out into society so more people understand it.

Recently JB's psychiatrist told us that we've done a great job with everything we're implementing, which is wonderful to hear. But we know our job isn't over and probably never will be.

Although we feel we have a nice strategy right now, I accept that this could change at any time and we would have to reassess. We can't get complacent.

Where are we now?

We are fortunate that we can work with JB to ensure his school work remains above where it needs to be. That way, if a problem does develop, we have time to work on it without him falling too far behind his classmates.

Currently, we don't medicate but haven't discounted that for the future if needed. We stay in constant contact with the school about his progress so we can assess at any time whether to consider medication. I would love to get JB through his life without it, but I know this may not be possible or the right choice for him later in life. It's something we remain open about.

I've started a business offering support to other parents of ADHD children and face-to-face support groups. I was inspired to do this after learning the amount of support that parents need and the total lack of support that's available.

I plan to advocate for all children living with ADHD, primarily to get government funding for schools so they can get the support they need to help these children.

This year, I've been very proud to be a contributing author on a book called *Parenting a Child on the Spectrum*[9], as well as speaking to audiences and running retreats. (I'd also love to run events for children living with ADHD and the siblings who are affected as well. But I'm still working on that idea.)

It seems my whole life is now devoted to advocating for ADHD and it all began with that trip to the director's office.

Beyond the ADHD label

Despite my current focus on ADHD, I see my son first and foremost as the person he is rather than the label he's been given by specialists.

That's why we've chosen not to tell JB that he lives with ADHD until he's older.

He knows he thinks differently; he says so himself. And that's fine for now. I tell him it's great to think differently, as that's how things change in the world—by people thinking differently.

We don't allow the word 'can't' in our vocabularies, believing that anything is possible if we set our minds to it. We wouldn't want him to feel he's unable to do something because he's been labelled with ADHD.

He will always be the wonderful, bright, witty person that he is and achieve great things despite the label.

Where are we now?

What you can do right now

So you're still in the thick of it and the struggle is real. What can you do right now to make things easier?

Spread the love

You love your child no matter what, right? Well, never let them forget that. Just reading this book shows that you want to accept ADHD for something other than what people tell you it is.

So even when your child is testing your patience to the max, remind them that you love them. Quite often, I'll say to JB, 'I love you but I'm not liking this behaviour right now' or 'I know you're having a problem controlling your behaviour at the moment and I get that, but it doesn't mean I have to like it, but I do still love you'.

These kids feel really out of control at this time, and reminding them that you love them no matter what might be just enough to help them through it.

Get help!

Don't try to do this on your own. It's really hard! Ask for help. Find someone who's good with your child and ask them to help you out. Can they take your child to the park while you take time out for an hour? Or can they simply come and sit with them while you go for a walk?

You need to look after yourself because, if you don't, who will? You need to be strong and supportive for them.

Let the small stuff go

If you have to get things done when your child goes to bed, that's what you have to do. A perfect house isn't a necessity (and I need reminding of this regularly!), so just get the bare essentials done if that's all you can do. Again, enlist help from family if you can or ask them take your child so you can get things done. Make sure everyone in the family is pulling their weight—don't feel you have to do it all yourself.

Be their advocate

Remember: If you're not their advocate, no one else will be. You need to push for help at school and outside of school. You need to support their friendships and encourage them. Without this, they will fall through the cracks of the system.

Be strong

If you let them, these kids will break you. Try to remain calm and know you're doing your best. This is *not* your fault. None of it is! It's the way their brain is wired and there's nothing you

Where are we now?

could have done to change that. So, if you are blaming yourself, stop! That will get you nowhere.

It's OK! You're doing an amazing job and you wouldn't have been chosen to be their parent if you couldn't handle it.

Beyond the ADHD Label
One Mother's Struggle for Change

Beyond the Maze

Paula is the owner of Beyond the Maze Pty Ltd, a parent advocate company backed by an advisory group comprising a psychologist, psychiatrist, animal therapist, nutritionist, occupational therapist, special needs teacher, paediatrician, naturopath, personal trainer, accountant and lawyer.

Paula regularly consults with her advisory board and seeks input from them about any new content she releases.

Beyond the Maze runs regular, free support groups and offers an annual membership to the website where you can keep up to date with changes in the industry, get discounts for upcoming events and participate in a private members forum. The company encourages a supportive, non-judgmental environment for all its members.

Beyond the Maze runs regular half-day workshops for parents who want to learn more about ADHD and an annual conference to provide access to specialists in one place. In the future, the company will also provide retreats for parents who

Beyond the ADHD Label
One Mother's Struggle for Change

need time out, fun events for kids living with ADHD, and events for siblings of children with ADHD.

Paula herself has plans to take on the education system and educate society about ADHD to facilitate a slightly easier journey for parents with children living with it.

She will also work with employers to create easier working environments for adults working with ADHD in the future.

Currently, Paula is visiting primary schools and community centres to educate parents on the strategies available for children living with ADHD. If you would like Paula to speak at your school or community event, please contact her team and organise an appointment.

If you don't have a support group nearby, contact the Beyond the Maze team to see what can be organised:

- website: www.beyondthemaze.com.au
- email: info@beyondthemaze.com.au
- phone: 1300 66 75 35.

Notes

1. David Giwerc & Barbara Luther, *Simply ADHD: Coach Training Manual*, ADD Coach Academy, 2013, pp. 40–44
2. Dr John Gray, *Staying Focused in a Hyper World: Book 1; Natural Solutions for ADHD, Memory and Brain Performance,* Amazon website: https://www.amazon.com.au/Staying-Focused-Hyper-World-Performance-ebook/dp/B00MC3SP78
3. The Chemical Maze, http://chemicalmaze.com/
4. Dr Ross W Greene, The Explosive Child: A New Approach for Understanding and Parenting Easily Frustrated, Chronically Inflexible Children, Amazon website: https://www.amazon.com/Explosive-Child-Understanding-Frustrated-Chronically/dp/0062270451
5. Sue Dengate, *Fed Up*, http://fedup.com.au/
6. Deakin University, *Dietetics FAQs*, http://www.deakin.edu.au/exercise-nutrition-sciences/careers/dietetics/dietetics-faqs

7. *Triple P: Positive Parenting Program,* http://www.triplep-parenting.net.au
8. *SleepTalk®,* http://www.sleeptalkchildren.com/
9. Deborah Fay and Lorna Emblen (compilers), *Parenting a Child on the Spectrum,* http://beyondthemaze.com.au/product/parenting-a-child-on-the-spectrum-printed-book/

www.ingramcontent.com/pod-product-compliance
Lightning Source LLC
Chambersburg PA
CBHW071707090426
42738CB00009B/1691